THE
elevation
APPROACH
WORKBOOK

ALSO BY THE AUTHOR

The Elevation Approach

THE
elevation
APPROACH
WORKBOOK

Practical Exercises and Everyday Tools to
Create Work-Life Harmony and
Accomplish Your Most Important Goals

TINA WELLS

with Stephanie Smith

RODALE

NEW YORK

Published in the United States by Rodale Books, an imprint of Random House,
a division of Penguin Random House LLC, New York.

RodaleBooks.com | RandomHouseBooks.com

RODALE and the Plant colophon are registered trademarks of
Penguin Random House LLC.

This work is based on and directly quotes from *The Elevation Approach* by Tina Wells with
Stephanie Smith, first published in hardcover by Rodale, an imprint of Random House, a
division of Penguin Random House LLC, New York, in 2023, copyright © 2023 by Tina
Wells.

ISBN 978-0-593-58026-4

Printed in the United States of America

Book design by Andrea Lau
Cover design by Irene Ng

1st Printing

First Edition

Contents

Introduction

Hi there!

I'm so glad you've made the powerful decision to elevate your life.

For most people, this means seeking out activities that align with your personal values and interests. Elevating your life can mean something different for each and every person picking up this book. Perhaps your life is great now. Perhaps you have a career you love and a home you enjoy. Your social life is thriving, and you find time to volunteer at a nonprofit or see friends regularly. For you, maybe elevating your life simply means having more time for the things you love to do or have been curious about doing for a while.

For others, maybe your life is okay, but there's something missing. You feel like you need to add something else to your routine, make a change that will create more joy, or seek something that will help you feel a sense of purpose. Maybe this something is a new job or a new hobby. Or maybe you want to change your surroundings, buy a new house, or move to a new neighborhood.

Elevating your life might also mean raising your physical or emotional baseline. Maybe you want to get healthier, improve your fitness level, or learn a new sport. Or maybe you just want to feel better—more at peace, more relaxed, and less frazzled or rushed. For me, elevation means living as my best self. When I feel my best, I move with ease from my work and family responsibilities to my hobbies and moments of self-care.

No matter how you define it, what matters is that your definition of elevation is relevant to you and your life. It's not about meeting other people's expectations or being the best, the first, the richest, or the most successful. Instead, you want to see how you can create a feeling of peace and contentment within yourself. What makes you breathe more easily? What makes you smile? What makes you feel like everything in your life is running smoothly?

Elevating your life can mean adding to or eliminating things from your plate. It can mean finding more time for or dedicating less time to an activity. It can mean discovering new experiences you had no idea existed. Elevation can come from a series of small steps, big decisions, or unexpected moves. No matter what your path looks like, you can make it happen. I'm here to show you how with the Elevation Approach.

The Elevation Approach is my method for creating work-life harmony. With this workbook, you'll have a pivotal tool that will help you use the Elevation Approach to make your biggest goals and wildest dreams a reality. As I shared in my book, *The Elevation Approach*, I created this four-phase plan to cultivate more of what I loved in life—more creativity, more joy, more flow. It changed my life, and I still use it to work through business challenges, reach personal goals, chase big dreams, and make small wishes come true.

Before developing the Elevation Approach, I already had lots of experience with problem-solving and goal setting. I launched my own business, Buzz Marketing Group, when I was sixteen. From there, I grew my small market research firm into an award-winning marketing agency with dozens of Fortune 500 clients. I was a successful CEO who earned spots on prominent young entrepreneur lists and magazine covers. I had tons of friends across the globe, including business founders and Hollywood celebrities, and even more memorable experiences from travels far and wide. I thought I had achieved that ideal work-life balance. While I dedicated myself to growing Buzz Marketing Group, I also found time to work out regularly at bootcamp classes, took vacations (albeit with laptop and cell phone in hand), and showed up for anyone who asked for my time.

But prioritizing my work-life balance didn't prevent me from burning out. I often sacrificed too much of my time and energy to satisfy others' needs or to reach my business goals. I felt like the hard work I put into maintaining my work and personal life wasn't resulting in the riches of life I'd imagined. Despite trying my hardest, I didn't have the ability to make my own schedule or do what I truly wanted to do. I didn't even always have the satisfaction that comes from working hard and doing good work.

After years of constantly working myself to exhaustion and resting only so that I could work even harder, I reached a breaking point. I knew I had to make a change in how I worked and lived. I wanted to figure out how I could juggle work, indulge my creativity, and enjoy my personal time without depleting myself. I wanted to make more room for rest and reflection. I wanted to spend time with family and appear in our photos instead of ducking out of special moments to check my emails or take a work call.

I started with this key shift: I prioritized work-life harmony instead of work-life balance. Next, I developed a system that would help me create work-life harmony. That's how the Elevation Approach was born. It's my way of taking action, prioritizing joy and ease, and moving forward with my goals in a fulfilling way. Once I revamped how I allocated my time and energy to my daily responsibilities, my life fell into a blissful rhythm in which I felt at peace, whether I was on vacation, at work, with friends, or at home alone.

If you've read my book *The Elevation Approach*, you are ready to dive into this workbook and recalibrate the way you conduct your daily life. You're familiar with what the Elevation Approach offers—what it is, how to use it, and how it's helped me. This workbook is designed to help you dig deeper into the method you've already practiced and give you a dedicated space in which to gather your ideas, thoughts, brainstorms, and moments of clarity and joy.

If you haven't read the book, don't worry. I'll give you a full overview of what the Elevation Approach is, how I've used it, and how it can help you elevate your life. You can then use this workbook to gain a head start on putting its principles into action today.

No matter where you're starting from, I want you to achieve the same work-life harmony in your life that I've finally obtained, where the things you do each day take your life to another level. The Elevation Approach is what has helped me achieve that goal in my life, and I hope it can move you toward the work-life harmony that feels good in your own life. All you have to do is stay open and come along with me as we move through the Elevation Approach so that you get closer to the bliss that this harmony brings.

Let me show you the way.

What Is the Elevation Approach?

The Elevation Approach is a flexible and adaptable method that helps you reach your goals while finding harmony between your work and your life along the way. It offers a cycle of activities that help you to make a plan, take action, create accountability, and think through challenges. You can use the Elevation Approach to tackle business and life goals, or to add more fun and joy to your life.

How It Works

The Elevation Approach consists of four phases. Here is a refresher of each phase and how these phases will help you reach your goals:

- **Preparation:** This is the time for planning. You'll gather the materials, tools, and resources that you need to get started and evaluate what you can realistically provide for your new project.

- **Inspiration:** This is where you seek out the books, images, places, and people that spark your creative energy. This is where you discover new ideas and open yourself to the world around you.

- **Recreation:** This is the phase where you take a break from your work. You'll indulge in a bit of fun to recharge, try activities that are unrelated to your goal, and allow yourself to take a breather.

- **Transformation:** This is the phase for reflection. You'll assess the work you've done so far, evaluate your results, determine how this work makes you feel, and note the progress you've made. Then you'll decide how you want to move forward.

Within each of the four phases you'll find three principles that offer what I like to call "instant elevation." These simple everyday actions, such as decluttering a workspace or creating a daily ritual, will bring you an immediate uplift while teaching you the skills that will help you create more work-life harmony. As I described in *The Elevation Approach*, you'll create practices, build systems, and strengthen the muscles you need to create work-life harmony. Not only will these new habits and small shifts bring individual moments of joy to your everyday life but they will also help you evaluate whether your day-to-day efforts are aligned with the other priorities, projects, and responsibilities in your life.

There are a few important features about the Elevation Approach. First, the Elevation Approach is cyclical. Each of the four phases flows from one to the next, and you can restart a new cycle of the Elevation Approach once you work through the last principle of the last phase, Transformation. Though Transformation is designed to be the point at which you assess where you are and where you want to go, it also serves as a springboard for restarting the Elevation Approach, beginning with the Preparation phase.

That said, you can start the Elevation Approach in whatever phase or principle you like. If you're starting a brand-new goal, the most natural place to begin the Elevation Approach would be the Preparation phase. If you're using the Elevation Approach to revisit an old goal that you haven't reached yet, jumping in at a different phase may be more useful. If you're picking up this workbook midway after you've started working on a goal, no sweat—select the phase where you think you should be and start from there. There are assessment questions at the end of each phase to help you reflect on the work you've accomplished. If you've already worked through the Elevation Approach a few times and are already familiar with the method, you might choose to focus on one phase because you're interested in practicing a specific principle. Feel free to dive into the phases and principles that best fit your current needs.

Finally, you can spend as much or as little time as you want in each phase. For example, perhaps you need to spend more time in Preparation because your goal requires you to learn new skills, but you choose to move through the Inspiration phase quickly because you've already gathered some sources for new ideas. Or perhaps you're already in the process of working toward your goal—say, you're taking a class you've signed up for before starting the Elevation Approach, and you're knee-deep in studying and learning. You may not need as much preparation or inspiration for the goal at hand, so you may spend more time in Recreation instead to give yourself some room to play and rest in between your studies.

Part of why I believe the Elevation Approach will help you achieve work-life harmony is that it's designed to be flexible and customizable. Just as the demands and responsibilities in your own life are constantly changing, the way in which you apply the Elevation Approach can also fluctuate, depending on what you need at a given time. There's no right way or wrong way to use my plan, and you don't need to give yourself a time constraint or daily deadlines to make it work for you. You can use the four phases and the twelve principles in ways that enhance your daily schedule or help you make progress toward anything you are trying to accomplish.

Create Work-Life Harmony

As I mentioned earlier, the key to revamping how I approached my work and life was to shift my focus from work-life balance to work-life harmony.

Work-life balance has become an outdated way of organizing our time and resources. Seeking a work-life balance forces you to take an either/or approach to these two important areas of your life. It assumes that your life is ideal when the time spent at work and the time spent outside of work are equal, and that it is always possible to split your time equally between the two. But that doesn't provide a framework for navigating the possibility that your work life will encroach on your personal life and vice versa. For example, you might need to take that conference call in the middle of your child's soccer game. You might discover that a close family member's wedding is scheduled for the same time as an important work presentation you're excited to lead.

Work-life balance also doesn't consider your emotions about work or work's emotional effects on your life, nor does it prevent you from taking on too many responsibilities. Trying to find a work-life balance encouraged me to find a way to do as much work and enjoy as much life as possible—an easy road to burnout. It gave me the impression that it was only possible to focus on one aspect of work or life at a time. It also made it difficult to consider the other aspects of life that needed my attention, such as my physical health, mental health, and relationships.

Under the guise of achieving a so-called balance, we've been multitasking and side-hustling our way to success for years, thinking that the harder we worked, the more likely we'd be able to pursue the things we really wanted to do later on. But this way of moving through life has made us more exhausted than ever before. Plus, life is short! Why postpone joy to a later date, especially when you're already working so hard?

In a postpandemic, globally focused world, we need to completely shift how we organize our lives, and that shift begins by unsubscribing from work-life balance and turning our attention to work-life harmony. Work-life harmony is better suited for the type of lives we're all living now, in which technology and remote jobs allow us to work where we want and sometimes when we want. Where people are forging their own careers by exploring their personal interests and showcasing their work on social media. Where people are prioritizing self-care and looking for more experiences that nurture their health and happiness.

Work-life harmony makes it possible to do all this and more, allowing us to fill our days with work, everyday responsibilities, and hobbies, as well as the big dreams and fun activities that bring fulfillment and give you a sense of purpose without sacrificing personal well-being. Work-life harmony results in a more satisfying life than work-life balance because it puts you and your interests first. It helps you align the responsibilities of your own life around your own priorities at a given time. If work must come first because you have a big deadline, you can easily shift your focus to this part of your life. But if taking care of an elderly family member suddenly becomes a must, you can change your priorities to give your loved one more of your attention.

Work-life harmony also helps you sync your life's purpose with your work and personal pursuits and permits you to easily adapt these pursuits as your needs and interests change. It allows you to take a look at your entire life and notice how its different parts work (or conflict) with one another. And once you understand how your days look now, work-life harmony will help you prioritize the tasks that bring personal fulfillment and satisfaction. For example, you can work all day, if that brings you joy, or you can fit surfing into your daily life, whether that means adjusting your workday to allow for a surf session in the morning or evening or watching big-wave documentaries while you prepare dinner for your family. In all these scenarios, you don't have to choose just work or a personal passion—you can find a way to fit both into your life in a manner that makes sense in your circumstances. Whatever choice you make, you'll know that you have work-life harmony when you feel that you can attend to all your life's priorities with intention and care.

Why a Workbook?

In *The Elevation Approach* book, I explain my story and share examples of how my method worked for me. In this workbook, the focus is on you, your journey, and your story. I created this workbook because I wanted to give you as many resources as possible to help you elevate your life. It's one thing to dictate a course of action and ask readers to follow your lead; it's another thing to give someone practical tools to help them thrive.

Like the book itself, this workbook will take you through one complete cycle of the Elevation Approach, explaining every phase and principle and how they work. You'll start by assessing what work-life harmony means to you. Next, you'll pinpoint the goal you will pursue for this cycle.

You'll then work through the four phases of the cycle at your own pace. At the beginning of each phase and principle, you'll find affirmations and key quotes from *The Elevation Approach* that will give you some words of encouragement. The quotes that kick off each principle will also remind you of the most important takeaways from each section and will provide a sense of purpose for the exercises ahead. The workbook's exercises will give you the opportunity to practice the lessons you learn and will empower you to take steps toward your goals. You'll try some of the activities included in *The Elevation Approach* and find new writing prompts, affirmations, and tasks that will inspire you to create work-life harmony and prioritize joy, no matter what phase you're in. Some exercises are designed to help you make consistent progress, celebrate successes, record new insights or thoughts that arise, or find solutions to remove obstacles. Others are more specific to a principle or phase. For example, you'll find exercises that will help you track data relevant to your goal or incorporate more movement into your day. The workbook also includes plenty of space to reflect on your experiences as you move through the process.

The workbook activities range in intensity. You can complete some exercises in a minute or two, while others might require more time or ask you to set your workbook down, complete a task, and return to its pages to reflect on your experiences. If you have a long-term goal and need to spend more time in a particular phase or principle, feel free to do so. If you're working through a short-term goal and need less time, then move as quickly as you like. Your experience with this workbook can be tailored to meet your needs.

I hope this workbook will be a place you can return to whenever you need guidance, support, or to check in with your feelings. As you work with the Elevation Approach, use this workbook to create a record of your journey. As we move through life, it's easy to get so focused on the results of our work that we don't take enough time to notice how we feel as we do the work. This workbook not only lets you reflect while you're working through the Elevation Approach, but it also allows you to refer back to your recollections and see what insights you discover in revisiting them.

The Elevation Approach helps you find the work-life harmony you deserve by ensuring that all the different parts of your life work together. With the help of this workbook, you'll find the things that light you up to create a life that shines. When you're faced with a crossroads, are focused on an important goal, or are excited by a big idea, these exercises can help you make decisions about what to do next and know that you've made the right choices.

getting started

"

Today I begin a new
chapter of my life
with limitless
possibilities.

"

In this chapter, you'll kick off the Elevation Approach with some exercises that are designed to help you think about where you are currently with your life. You'll name the things you want or aspire to be, and you'll outline an attainable goal. The exercises will also help you discover why this goal is important to you, how the goal will impact your life, and how you'd like to achieve this goal.

In this section, you'll complete the following tasks:

- Write down any feelings or thoughts you have before diving into the Elevation Approach. Are you feeling nervous about starting something new? Are you scared of confronting some of the stumbling blocks or fears you've had about reaching for a big goal?

- Imagine what your ideal harmonious day is like. What does your daily routine look like? What things are you doing? Where are you? How much work, free time, recreational activities, and family time constitute your day? Think through what elements of your life make up a harmonious day and what you think, feel, and do (maybe even eat!) during that process.

- Write down the elevated goal you want to achieve via the Elevation Approach, using the SMART goal framework.

- Declare your commitment to follow the Elevation Approach and reach your goal.

Take as much time as you like with these exercises. You may find it easier to start with one exercise at a time, or you might prefer to complete them in one sitting. It's up to you.

Journey Journal

Before we get started, take some time to jot down your feelings and thoughts as you go into the Elevation Approach. Here, think about what emotions, concerns, hopes, and dreams come to mind as you begin, then respond to the following prompts.

How do you want to feel every day?

_____

_____

_____

_____

_____

_____

_____

_____

_____

_____

What are your most important goals?

_____

_____

_____

_____

_____

_____

_____

_____

_____

_____

What does work-life harmony feel like to you?

_____

_____

_____

_____

_____

_____

_____

_____

_____

_____

_____

_____

What will help you live a more joyous life?

_____

_____

_____

_____

_____

_____

_____

_____

_____

_____

_____

_____

Draw Your Day

If you looked at my calendar and saw how I organized an average day in my life, you'd notice how my time blocks correspond to the phases of the Elevation Approach. My mornings are spent preparing: reading, listening to podcasts, or cooking. Afterward, I move into the Inspiration part of my day. I take meetings and calls, becoming more visible and social. Around mid-afternoon, it's time for Recreation. On my breaks, I try to find time for a walk or an opportunity to sit outside for fifteen minutes, feel the sun, and breathe clean air. Then I transition to Transformation and tackle the more reflective or analytical tasks in the later afternoon. By the evening, I feel rested, productive, and ready to tackle the next day.

My ideal day draws from the phases of the Elevation Approach, but what about you? What part of your day do you want to spend on your hobby? When do you want to work out or get some other physical activity? When do you want to work or feel most productive?

Using this clock diagram, map out how you currently spend your typical day. Be as detailed as possible and include all the activities you can think of, such as watching television, working, exercising, eating meals, and sleeping.

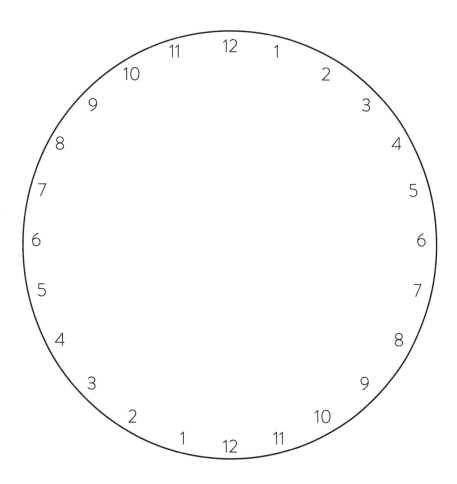

With this clock diagram, map out how you would like to spend your ideal day. Include everything you consider a top priority, such as quality time with family, hobbies, or fun social gatherings. Don't forget to include time for rest!

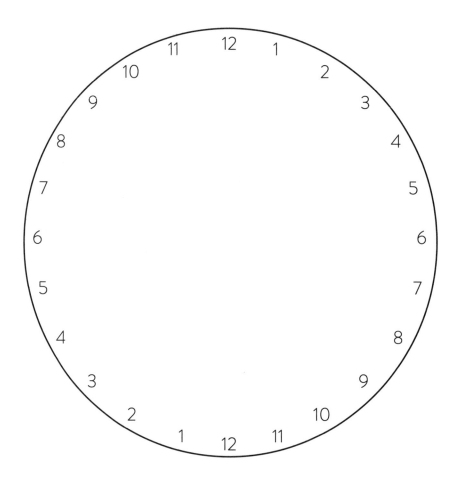

Now, compare and contrast the two diagrams you've made with these prompts. Responding to these prompts will help you start thinking about where you can make more time for the top priorities in your life.

Do you think you've allotted enough time in each day to complete all your responsibilities?

_____

_____

_____

_____

_____

_____

Are you spending too much time on some areas of your life? What makes you feel this way?

_____

_____

_____

_____

_____

_____

In what areas would you like to spend more time?

_____

_____

_____

_____

_____

_____

What is something you included in your ideal day that is missing from your current day?

_____

_____

_____

_____

_____

_____

_____

_____

_____

_____

_____

Is there anything missing from both diagrams that you'd like to find time for?

_____

_____

_____

_____

_____

_____

_____

_____

_____

_____

_____

_____

Name Your Goal

In the previous exercise, you diagramed your ideal day. Now, let's think about how you can apply the Elevation Approach to incorporate parts of your ideal day into your typical day.

First, take a breath. You don't need to overhaul your entire life in a short amount of time. You will not upend everything you know simply for the sake of trying something new. Change is good, but changing everything all at once can be overwhelming.

This is why I recommend choosing one goal that will improve your life and following one complete cycle of the Elevation Approach to work toward this goal. Start with one goal that will have a measurable impact on your day-to-day life—something that will enhance your life, not create more stress or frustration. Think of a goal that will make you smile more, help you feel more content, and have a lasting impact.

Got something in mind? Good. Use the space that follows to jot down a brief description of your goal and explain why this goal is important to you.

Describe your goal.

_____

_____

_____

_____

Why do you want to pursue this goal?

_____

_____

_____

_____

_____

How will your daily life change as you work toward this goal? What might you have to pull back from to move closer to this goal?

_____

_____

_____

_____

_____

_____

_____

What will you gain if you accomplish the goal?

_____

_____

_____

_____

_____

_____

_____

When you accomplish the goal, how will your life be different in one month from now? In six months? In one year?

_____

_____

_____

_____

_____

_____

_____

Feeling good about your goal? Great. Now let's get as specific as possible about what that goal is and how you're going to accomplish it.

To get the most out of the Elevation Approach, it's best to define your goal clearly. A popular way to do this is to use the SMART goal framework. SMART is an acronym, where each letter stands for an important quality that every goal should have: Specific, Measurable, Achievable, Relevant, and Time-based. Outlining any goal using these elements will allow you to describe in more detail what your goal is, what you need to do to achieve it, and how much time it will take for you to get there.

For example, let's explore how the SMART framework might look if your goal is to apply to graduate school:

- **Specific:** I want to earn a master's degree in my field of work.
- **Measurable:** I will choose five schools with programs that fit my interests and apply to each one.
- **Achievable:** I can finish the master's program in less than two years and can take time from work to attend classes.
- **Relevant:** The master's degree will give me more long-term job security. I will earn more money in my industry and be able to teach at a college level in the future.
- **Time-based:** I will work on my applications and have all five ready to send in four weeks.

Now it's your turn! Using the worksheet that follows, describe the goal you're trying to reach and the information that corresponds to each column. How will you measure the success of your goal? How will you reach that goal? Why is the goal relevant to you? How much time will it take you to reach that goal? Be as specific as possible with your answers.

After you've filled in the columns, refine the description of your goal that you wrote on page 21. Incorporate the details you shared on this worksheet into the updated description.

As you work through the Elevation Approach, feel free to revisit this page often to remind yourself of the specific goal and the parameters you set for reaching the goal.

S

M

A

R

T

~~~~~~~~~~~~~~~~~~~~~~~~~~

GOAL

COMPLETED BY

Commit to Work-Life Harmony

You've already decided that your goal is important and achieving it will make your life better. Now you'll commit to doing the work toward reaching that goal.

Make a contract with yourself using the following pledge and promise to dive into the Elevation Approach with an open mind and good intentions. Your pledge will remind you of the commitment you're making to yourself to create work-life harmony in your life!

Review this statement, fill in your name, and sign your pledge.

MY COMMITMENT TO WORK-LIFE HARMONY

I, _____, commit to cultivating and bringing work-life harmony into my life, and pursuing this goal to

_____

will help me achieve more harmony in my life. I will move forward with a positive attitude and hope for the best. I will expand my curiosity about the good that awaits me. I will be open to new ideas and possibilities. I will be honest with myself about my feelings. I will reflect often on my progress, and I will seek help and rest, if needed.

Above all, I will believe I can make any dream, any goal, any plan, come to fruition if I put my mind to it.

In harmony,

_____

Signature

_____

Date

PHASE ONE

preparation

Affirmation

"

I am clearing
space for a new
approach to life
that puts my
joy first.

"

Preparation is the natural first step in kicking off any program, scheme, or project, including the Elevation Approach. This is the phase in which you begin creating a plan for reaching your goal and get yourself ready to tackle it. You outline exactly what you will need to get going, from the gear you'll need to buy to the people you can turn to for help. You get your mind focused on the goal at hand. You prepare your space—both the physical and the mental ones—to make room for the materials you'll gather and the new ideas to come. If needed, you'll prepare your finances and decide how much money to allocate to your goal. You prepare your spirit as well, taking stock of where you are so you can see where you want to be.

In the Preparation phase, you will learn about these three principles: **declutter your spaces, get curious,** and **know your numbers.**

- When you declutter, you'll clear out old, unused goods or items to make room for the things you'll need to achieve your goal. You'll take stock not only of your physical clutter but of your mental, digital, and schedule clutter as well.

- When you get curious, you'll ask yourself about the great things that might come from pursuing your goal. Instead of turning your attention toward what you can't or shouldn't do, you'll think about the exciting opportunities that come to mind when you ask yourself, "What if . . . ?" or "Wouldn't it be great if . . . ?"

- And finally, a pivotal part of preparation is knowing your numbers. You'll learn how to gather facts and figures about your goal and track your progress. You'll also assess your current situation, statistics, balances, and standings.

At the end of this phase, you'll have hard data and clear facts in regard to where you currently stand in relationship to your goal and what you'll need to help you achieve your goal. Knowledge is power; here, knowledge will give you confidence and propel you into action.

To get yourself ready to take on the Preparation phase, you'll work on the following activities:

- Write down any thoughts or feelings you have as you're about to dive in.

- Create a vision statement and define success on your own terms.

- Define your nonnegotiables to determine what you refuse to sacrifice in reaching your goal.

- Build a tool kit to help you assess what you need to start working on your goal.

Types of Preparation

- **Mental preparation:** Mental preparation means getting into the most powerful mindset for achieving your goal. Where the mind goes, the body will follow. You need to believe it's possible to achieve your goals. You need to trust that the work you'll do will pay off. You'll also need to get real about where you are—give yourself a reality check if something's not working and answer some hard questions. What becomes possible if you reach your goal? What needs to change for you to make progress?

- **Physical preparation:** Assess what equipment, materials, or tools are needed to work on your goal. Do you have a designated space where you will work toward your goal—for example, a desk, a room, or a studio? What does your workspace look like for accomplishing the new activities you want to take on? Does the space need any rearranging or any new accessories or tools before you dive into your new goal? Is there anything you can do to make it more inspiring and inviting?

- **People preparation:** You'll gather the people you'll want to surround yourself with as you move toward your goal. These people can include close friends and family, colleagues, or professionals, as well as casual acquaintances who can help you, share advice, or offer support. We'll dive deeper into strengthening these connections in the Inspiration phase (see Principle #5: Build Your Tribe, page 99).

- **Data preparation:** With any goal, it's important to know your stats. If you're looking to run faster, you need to know how fast you run now and how much you need to increase your speed. If you're trying to save more money, you need to know how much is in your account now and how much more you should save. Gathering as much quantitative information as possible about your goal will help you understand what it will take to reach that goal. We'll discuss this more in the chapter covering Principle #3: Know Your Numbers, page 65).

- **Financial preparation:** Determine how much it might cost to work on your goal and how you will allocate funds.

- **Schedule preparation:** Make a regular date with yourself to work on your goal. You might need to move your schedule around, delegate some of your responsibilities to others, or say no to other commitments.

Journey Journal

Before we get started with the Preparation phase, take some time in the space that follows to jot down any feelings and thoughts you have as you begin this phase. Here are some prompts for you to ponder:

What doubts, fears, and worries are preventing you from reaching your goal? How can you tune out those feelings to focus on reaching your goal?

_____

_____

_____

_____

_____

_____

_____

_____

_____

Do you have a dedicated workspace? How can you prepare that space to support your work with the Elevation Approach?

_____

_____

_____

_____

_____

_____

_____

_____

_____

Take stock of the resources you have to work on your goal. Do you feel that you have the support you need? Which areas will you need help with?

_____

_____

_____

_____

_____

_____

_____

_____

_____

_____

_____

_____

What excites you the most about starting the Elevation Approach?

_____

_____

_____

_____

_____

_____

_____

_____

_____

_____

_____

Craft Your Vision Statement

When I give business advice to aspiring entrepreneurs, I recommend they create a vision statement. A vision statement defines your vision for yourself and your life. It allows you to explain the reasons behind why you do what you do.

For example, I have made a promise to myself to carve out fifteen minutes of my morning just for myself. I am so committed to this routine that I wake up at 5:30 a.m. every day just to ensure I get this time alone, without distractions—no emails, no texts, no outside noise. This "me time" allows me to go forth into my day feeling calm and centered. I also use that time to envision the greatest possibilities that day can bring.

Here is how I've crafted a vision statement to express my commitment to set aside those precious minutes for myself every morning:

I, Tina Wells, will preserve fifteen minutes just for myself every morning. I will wake up at 5:30 a.m. (or as early as necessary) to ensure I start my day with no distractions or interruptions. I will hold a vision of what the best possible version of my day could look like. I will not tune in to any work or personal responsibilities until after I've enjoyed this time to myself. This time is valuable to me because it will allow me to start my day grounded and relaxed, and in a better mental state to take on whatever is in store for the day.

Now it's your turn to create a personal vision statement. In the space that follows, explain what your personal vision for your life is and how your goal fits into this vision. Explain why your goal is something you want. Be specific, but think big!

Name Your Nonnegotiables

Inevitably, you'll run into situations in which you have to choose between doing tasks that move you toward your goal and tasks that direct your energy to other parts of your life. With the Elevation Approach, you don't need to sacrifice your health or anything else related to your self-preservation to achieve something, nor do you need to spend less time on your personal interests or fun diversions. There should be some parts of your life you shouldn't have to give up, no matter what.

In this exercise, you'll define your nonnegotiables—the tasks, hobbies, and responsibilities you refuse to give up. Having guardrails around what you won't sacrifice will allow you to preserve time and energy for the things that are most important to you. Sure, achieving an important goal is great, but doing so at the expense of what you love most won't make that accomplishment as satisfying.

Knowing your nonnegotiables also keeps you from over-exhausting yourself, to the point where you forgo the habits that keep you healthy and thriving. Maintaining your self-care rituals (for example, eating a healthy breakfast), or the routines that help you function better (think regular meditation or turning off electronics an hour before bed), or the activities that simply feel good (calling a family member who makes you laugh once a day or playing a silly game with your children) will prevent burnout.

A nonnegotiables list could include such things as a good night's sleep or a clean place to live. You can mention something as small as your morning cup of coffee or something as personally meaningful as tucking your kids into bed at night.

Consider what things you want on your nonnegotiables list. What limits will you put in place as you move forward with your goal? The items on your list can relate to your emotional, physical, or financial needs or can prioritize specific people or social commitments.

Then think about how you will protect the time and energy you devote to your nonnegotiables. What are ways you can reserve your time or resources? The more specific your strategies, the better.

Your Personal Nonnegotiables:

1. _____
   _____

2. _____
   _____

3. _____
   _____

4. _____
   _____

5. _____
   _____

Nonnegotiables Preservation Tactics:

1. _____
   _____

2. _____
   _____

3. _____
   _____

4. _____
   _____

5. _____
   _____

Build Your Tool Kit

It's important to know what tools you'll need to tackle your goals. On pages 30–31, you reviewed several different ways you can prepare for your goal. Here, you will get a kick-start on doing that with this physical, people, and financial preparation.

Gather Your Tools

In the space that follows, list the key tools, goods, gear, and training you'll need to reach your goal. You can write down both the things you already own and the things you'll need to acquire. Then check one of the boxes to the right of each item to designate whether you need to source the item and, if so, how you'll do so.

After completing this exercise, you will have an idea of what tools you'll need to gather and make room for. This will be especially helpful when you work on the first principle of the Elevation Approach: Declutter Your Spaces (page 45).

ITEM	OWN	BORROW	BUY
	☐	☐	☐
	☐	☐	☐
	☐	☐	☐
	☐	☐	☐
	☐	☐	☐
	☐	☐	☐
	☐	☐	☐
	☐	☐	☐
	☐	☐	☐
	☐	☐	☐
	☐	☐	☐
	☐	☐	☐
	☐	☐	☐
	☐	☐	☐
	☐	☐	☐
	☐	☐	☐
	☐	☐	☐
	☐	☐	☐

Gather Your People

Take stock of the people you want to have on call, ready to help you achieve your goal. Who might have the expertise you need? Who has successfully done what you are hoping to achieve? Who might be that great cheerleader to help you stay motivated or a good person to listen to you when you need a sympathetic ear? Who can hold you accountable and check in on your progress?

In the blank address book that follows, write down the names of the people who come to mind, what role they might play, and their contact information. Include everyone, from your close friends to the teachers or professionals you may need to consult for their expertise.

NAME: _____   NAME: _____

ROLE: _____   ROLE: _____

EMAIL: _____   EMAIL: _____

PHONE: _____   PHONE: _____

NAME: _____   NAME: _____

ROLE: _____   ROLE: _____

EMAIL: _____   EMAIL: _____

PHONE: _____   PHONE: _____

NAME: _____   NAME: _____

ROLE: _____   ROLE: _____

EMAIL: _____   EMAIL: _____

PHONE: _____   PHONE: _____

Gather Your Money

Knowing how much money you'll need to invest in your goal is vital. It helps you better understand how much you may need to save and how to allocate your funds, especially if you're on a tight budget.

But financial preparation isn't just about knowing how much your goal will cost; it's also about knowing how much it can add to your life. And that value isn't always stated in dollars. For example, if your goal is to buy a more fuel-efficient car, the value in that purchase might come from the savings on gasoline but it could also come from decreasing your carbon footprint or adopting an eco-friendlier lifestyle.

Using the worksheet that follows, list the expenses related to your goal. Think about how much it might cost you to obtain the goal and be sure to include any upfront costs, such as fees for classes or equipment. Then think through how much value reaching the goal can provide, whether it's an immediate cash payout, any savings in time, or something more intangible. Also, though we encourage you to quantify as much of your goal as possible, consider the nonmonetary value of your goal, especially one that will bring significant emotional value to your life.

Here is an example of how you might fill out the worksheet if, say, your goal is to replace your current vehicle with an electric car:

EXPENSE	COST	FREQUENCY OF EXPENSE
Car payment	$550	Monthly
Car insurance payment	$150	Monthly
Vehicle registration costs	$150	Annually
Charging costs	$50	Monthly

Value/Savings:

- Selling old car, $10,000

- Cost of gasoline, $200/month

- Cheaper maintenance, $460/annually (over 10 years)

- Satisfaction of driving a fuel-efficient, environmentally friendly car

Now, fill in the worksheet with your particular expenses.

EXPENSE	COST	FREQUENCY OF EXPENSE

Value/Savings

- _____
- _____
- _____
- _____
- _____
- _____

Your Personal Elevation Page

In the Preparation phase, you've started to gather materials, organize your spaces, and catalog what you need and want to protect. Now, using this space, take some time to jot down any uplifting moments, ideas, or images you'll want to remember. You can also use this space to keep any important information related to your prep work. There are no rules here, just space for you to express yourself.

Declutter Your Spaces

instant elevation

**By decluttering, you are sending a clear signal
to the world (and yourself) that you are ready to start something new.**

It's hard to start something new if your space feels cluttered and messy. In order to bring in and explore fresh ideas, you need to clean out the old gunk first.

Clutter is anything that creates negative feelings and prevents us from focusing on our tasks, because that clutter is misplaced or unwanted. It's stuff that gets in the way. We all have certain types of clutter that tend to pile up when we're moving at the speed of life:

- **Physical clutter,** or the stuff we accumulate. This can be clothing, furniture, kitchenware, food storage containers, unopened mail, sporting equipment—or anything else that piles up in your spaces.

- **Mental clutter,** or the thoughts, worries, concerns, and desires that distract and distress us.

- **Digital clutter,** or the apps, documents, photos, and notifications on our devices that overwhelm us.

- **Calendar clutter,** or the tasks, meetings, and other commitments that make us feel overscheduled.

Clutter isn't just an eyesore. It's also often a sign that you might not be paying attention to something important in your life. Eventually, you might hit your "clutter trigger point"—the threshold where clutter becomes impossible to ignore. Clutter can often accumulate because you're devoting more of your attention to some areas of your life over others. When you declutter your spaces, you give yourself the opportunity to reset and clear away anything that is distracting you from what you want to focus on.

Clearing out clutter also helps you make space for the things you really want in your life. By decluttering, you make sure your physical, mental, and digital spaces, as well as your calendar, have room for the new opportunities, routines, and other things that truly bring you joy. You also send a signal to yourself and the world that you're ready to start something new, that you're ready to receive new ideas, results, or blessings.

Here, you will complete a few exercises that can help you tackle these different types of clutter and recognize how and why clutter ends up accumulating in the first place.

Declutter Your Physical Space

In this exercise, you'll declutter the workspace you've set aside for reaching your goal. You'll remove unneeded items that are taking up space and clear off any important surfaces.

How to Put Physical Clutter in Its Place

1. Remove any items you don't need from the space.
2. Assign any remaining items to these three categories: keep, toss, or donate. Keep what you need, toss what you don't, and donate what you can to others.
3. Return "keep" items to their proper homes in your space, whether it's a desktop, pen holder, drawer, bookshelf, or organizer.
4. Create a plan for keeping clutter to a minimum. If some of your items don't have a home, can you find one for them? Can you create clutter-free zones with baskets, file organizers, closets, holders, or trays to gather the items? Can you build systems with folders or other organizational tools to create order and gather items that are often disorganized?

Declutter DJ

Decluttering doesn't have to be a chore if you make it fun. Choose a favorite playlist or album to keep you company as you declutter. If you're working on a small space, choose two or three songs; if you're tackling a large room, ten or so songs might be necessary.

You can even use your soundtrack to turn decluttering into a game. For each song, designate a small area or surface in your room or space that you're decluttering. Then press Play and try to clear this area before the song ends. For example, if you're decluttering a bedroom, use one song to organize a bedroom dresser, the next song to clean out your jewelry box, and so on and so forth. Use the space that follows to create your decluttering playlist.

My Decluttering Playlist

1. _____
2. _____
3. _____
4. _____
5. _____
6. _____
7. _____
8. _____
9. _____
10. _____

Now, let's reflect on where clutter comes from and then create a clutter-prevention plan. Using the "Clutter Recap" prompts that follow, pinpoint which areas in your workspace are your clutter hot zones and observe when the clutter begins to bother you. Then using the questions in the "Clutter Prevention Plan" section that follows next, create a system to keep clutter away—be it a system of organization to prevent you from leaving things out or a routine to gather and organize your things.

CLUTTER RECAP

What is your most cluttered area? What items are taking up too much space?

_____

_____

_____

_____

_____

How would you like those areas to look and feel?

_____

_____

_____

_____

_____

What are your clutter trigger points?

_____

_____

_____

_____

_____

Why do you think the clutter gathered to a point of disarray? For example, are you lacking time to organize? Do you not have enough space to store your stuff?

_____

_____

_____

_____

_____

CLUTTER PREVENTION PLAN

What systems can you put into place to avoid clutter?

_____

_____

_____

_____

_____

List any tools you can use with your plan, such as racks, organizers, baskets, or boxes.

_____

_____

_____

_____

_____

Declutter Your Mental Space

Many of us can store a complex amount of information in our brain at any one time. But too much information, especially information we don't necessarily need to act on at a given time, can lead to mental clutter. Mental clutter comprises the many thoughts, worries, and distractions that pass through our mind. It's all the unnecessary stuff that distracts and distresses us. Sometimes, these thoughts can leave us paralyzed, unable to think clearly enough to make decisions or to take action, especially when we're trying to get started on a goal.

Too much on our mind can make us feel overwhelmed and anxious. It also takes up brainpower that we might otherwise use for the things we really want to use it for. Decluttering your mind gives you a break from thinking about the superfluous, whether that's what you will make for dinner or what will happen if you break your leg, and will help you focus on what you really need to make progress.

In this meditation exercise, you'll visualize putting away your worries, doubts, and stray thoughts. This is a great exercise to do before taking on something creative. Oftentimes, the fear of not producing something perfect or popular will paralyze you from forging ahead. For example, thoughts such as *I'm not as good as everyone else!* or *I don't have the perfect social connections so I can't launch a business* can stop us from getting started. Let go of these judgments by following these steps:

1. Sit in a comfortable place with your back straight. Relax your body. Try not to touch any objects that can restrict movement.
2. Close, or relax, your eyes. Take a few deep breaths. Think about how you want to feel in this moment. Relaxed? Calm? Focused?
3. Take one of the thoughts occupying your mind and visualize putting the thought into a box. Repeat this visualization with any other distracting thoughts.
4. When you're finished, "pack up" the box, sealing those worrisome thoughts and feelings inside, and move the box outside of your mind.

5. When you're ready, open your eyes and gently begin to come back into your space.

You could repeat this exercise, applying it to other areas of your life where such thoughts might be on your mind. Continue to pack up any worries, whether they be about your family, your health, or something else, and place those worries in the box. Then breathe slowly and deeply as you imagine yourself moving it outside of your mind.

Brain Dump

Here's another chance to get all the worries, thoughts, and distractions out of your mind before you dive into the Elevation Approach. Do a brain dump by writing down anything on your mind. Don't edit or spell-check—just write! Imagine you've turned on a spigot in your brain and all your thoughts begin to flow out onto this page.

Once you've got all those thoughts out of your brain, you'll be ready to tackle your goal with a clear head.

_____

_____

_____

_____

_____

_____

_____

_____

_____

_____

_____

_____

_____

_____

_____

_____

_____

_____

_____

_____

_____

_____

_____

Declutter Your Calendar

One of the simplest ways to find time to work on your goal is to add it to your calendar. You've already outlined your ideal day in the exercise on page 18. In this exercise, you'll look at your weekly schedule and track what you've done in the past seven days by using the handy scheduler on the next page. As with the earlier Draw Your Day exercise, make sure to include everything you do—whether it's eating, sleeping, and working or looking at social media, socializing, exercising, or watching television.

When you're finished, return here and answer the following questions:

Are there any free blocks of time you can use for reaching your goal?

_____

_____

_____

_____

Consider how you can free up more time to work on your goal. Are there any tasks you can delegate or social commitments you can say no to?

_____

_____

_____

_____

_____

How can you protect the time you've dedicated to your goal?

_____

_____

_____

_____

MONTH / YEAR _____

	Sun ___	Mon ___	Tue ___	Wed ___	Thu ___	Fri ___	Sat ___
6 AM							
7 AM							
8 AM							
9 AM							
10 AM							
11 AM							
Noon							
1 PM							
2 PM							
3 PM							
4 PM							
5 PM							
6 PM							
7 PM							
8 PM							
9 PM							
10 PM							
11 PM							

Forward, Unsubscribe, Group, Delete

Do you have any files, documents, songs, photos, applications, and other data you no longer need? How about those pesky emails, advertisements for products you never open, software on your laptop you never use, or old e-receipts for products you bought years ago? This exercise will help you get your digital clutter under control.

Most apps, emails, photos, and digital files can be managed in one of four ways: forward, unsubscribe, group, or delete. For example, to manage the digital junk in your email inbox, forward important emails that need additional help or input from other people and group important emails (for example, tax receipts) you'd like to save into a folder. Unsubscribe from newsletters or lists that you no longer need and delete junk emails from your inbox.

Use the following tracker to see the impact of your decluttering. Write down the number of apps, emails, files, songs, and photos you have before and after decluttering. You'll feel a sense of accomplishment when you see the difference between the amount of digital stuff you had before and what you have after your decluttering session.

TYPE OF DIGITAL CLUTTER	BEFORE DECLUTTERING	AFTER DECLUTTERING
Apps		
Emails		
Files		
Songs		
Photos		

> **TIP:** Here's a way to quickly delete unwanted emails. Enter the word *subscribe* into the search bar of your email inbox. The emails that appear in the search results are likely from advertisements, flyers, or newsletters you've subscribed to over the years. Scan the results quickly, see which emails you haven't opened in a while, and unsubscribe from those mailing lists. Then group the results by sender and delete any outdated news alerts, promotions, and newsletters in bulk.

Get Curious

**Curiosity will help you look at the world
with a sense of hope and opportunity.**

Curiosity is an important fear-fighting and problem-solving tool, especially during the Preparation phase. When you start something new, you might feel scared or out of your depth. Curiosity can help you stay positive and feel more confident about your ability to do hard things.

Curiosity will help you look at the world with a sense of hope and opportunity. When you allow curiosity to guide your thinking, you'll find it easier to stay focused on the positive possibilities of your actions. Curiosity can encourage you to look beyond the familiar and help you support (or even discover) new passions.

Curiosity also helps you brainstorm solutions to challenging situations or unexpected problems. Perhaps you have had a negative way of thinking about your skills and abilities—for instance, I can't do something because I've never done it before. Questioning this thinking begins by asking "Why do I believe that?" or "What if I changed a few things about how I do something?" This curiosity might allow you to focus on solutions rather than feeling faced with roadblocks.

One great quality of curiosity is that it can be cultivated. Think of it as a muscle you can exercise. Asking more questions about your circumstances can help you gain new perspectives and make deeper connections to the world around you.

In this section, you'll find a few exercises that will help you develop curiosity, practice moving more slowly, and take time to be in the present. Let's dive in and see what happens when you begin to ask questions and then listen to your answers.

Play the "What If?" Game

One way to spark curiosity and reassure yourself when your doubts about reaching a goal or dream appear is to play the "What If?" game. This game helps focus your thoughts on the possibilities that could come with your actions. It encourages you to think what would happen if you do reach your goal, if those good things do happen, if your life changes for the better, and if it all works out.

The "What If?" game can also help you reframe some fears or worries you might have about your goal and the Elevation Approach. Say, you're afraid of flying and your goal is to try to overcome that fear. When you think about stepping onto a plane, your mind might drift to the possible disasters: What if there's turbulence? What if we crash? You can use this game to create positive scenarios instead; for example, What if we don't have turbulence? What if our flight goes smoothly? What if we make it to our destination early?

Here, you'll play this game with yourself. You'll brainstorm all the possible positive outcomes that could result from working through the Elevation Approach. You'll focus on those positive possibilities and reframe any fears that may have popped up, especially after completing the previous exercises.

Fill in the following sentences with a description of the good things that could come from your work. The bigger and brighter, the better!

What if _____?

What if _____?

What if _____?

What if _____?

What if _____?

What if _____?

What if _____?

What if _____?

What if _____?

Twenty Questions

Remember Twenty Questions, the game you might have played when you were a kid? This exercise is inspired by that concept. In the children's game, you use your curiosity to ask twenty questions that help you guess what someone is thinking about. Here, you'll ask yourself twenty questions about your goal, using your own sense of wonder to think through the possibilities of that goal and focus your mind on the work ahead.

For example, if your goal is to drink less alcohol, here are some questions you could ask:

- What would happen if I drank less alcohol?

- What else could I do with the cash I would save from not buying as much alcohol?

- What would I do with my time instead of going out for drinks after work or school?

- What if I swapped my glass of wine at the end of a long day with something else, such as a workout or a meditation break? How would my life improve?

- What if I give up drinking and meet someone whom I might not have gotten to know because they didn't drink?

What do you want to explore about yourself? What do you hope to learn? What answers are you trying to find?

1. _____
2. _____
3. _____
4. _____
5. _____
6. _____
7. _____

8. _____

9. _____

10. _____

11. _____

12. _____

13. _____

14. _____

15. _____

16. _____

17. _____

18. _____

19. _____

20. _____

Face Your Fears

It can be scary to start something new. Those fears can be big or small. For example, if you're moving to a new state, you might worry that you'll never see your family again, now that they are so far away, just as much as you fret about missing your old neighborhood deli.

If you're nervous or scared about some aspect of your goal, fight that fear by seeking more knowledge about the sources of your fear. When we feel fear, it's often because we don't know what the outcome of something is going to be or we don't have the important information about it. The more we know about a topic, situation, task, or activity, though, the less fear we are likely to have about it. Use your fears as a signal to seek out more information about what you're trying to do so that you can feel more comfortable and confident.

In the left column of the worksheet that follows, write down the fears—and be specific. What are you afraid of losing if you pursue your goal? What are you afraid of outgrowing or missing? Then in the right column, ask yourself what you can learn from those fears. What skills can you draw on to overcome that fear? What actions can you take to feel more empowered? How can you gather more information about your goal? And what personal lessons can you learn in the meantime?

If you need help getting started, take a look at the responses in the following sample:

GOAL: I would like to move to a new state.

FEAR	WHAT I CAN LEARN
I won't know anyone and won't have any friends.	I can learn how to make new friends or meet people with similar interests.
I don't know if I'll find work in the new place.	I can research local companies with open positions that allow me to apply my skills.
I won't be able to find a coffee shop/gym/grocery store I like.	I'll ask the locals for recommendations (and make more friends in the process).

FEAR	WHAT I CAN LEARN

Know Your Numbers

instant elevation

When you know your numbers, you have undeniable, quantifiable data that can inform your steps toward your goal.

With any goal, gathering data is essential for success. If you want to get healthier, learn a new skill, or take up a new hobby, understanding your important facts and numbers will allow you to assess where you are, what you need, and what constitutes success. When you have undeniable, quantifiable data, you can gain insights that will inform your plans.

It might be scary and intimidating at first to face the hard truth about where you stand now in relation to your goal, especially if you are further from it than you thought. It can sometimes be more comfortable to tell yourself a softer version of the facts. For example, when examining your finances, you might have thought, *I don't spend that much money* or *I'm not that much in debt.* But knowing specific numbers about your money matters—how much you owe on each credit card, what the outstanding balance on your mortgage is, how much you're spending on a weekly basis for food, clothing, and rent—is what will help you realize exactly your financial situation. From there, you can devise a strategy that can help you manage your money more effectively. As tough as it can be to face your numbers, the information they provide will spark change and force you to get real about where you are and where you want to be.

The exercises in this section will help you figure out exactly where you stand in relation to your goal and what you need to do to reach it. Knowing your numbers is powerful knowledge you can use to make wise decisions, solve problems, and figure out your next steps. By the end of the last exercise, those numbers should help you feel more confident about what you're doing and why.

How to Quantify Qualitative Data

With some goals, it might be easy to quantify what progress and success look like. With others, though, it might be hard to figure out how data can serve as your guide. If you have a goal that's hard to quantify, try these strategies:

- **Think in terms of time.** Deciding how much time you'd like to devote to your goal and then tracking the hours you put into it are simple ways to hold yourself accountable. For example, if you want to take up rowing, you might decide that you'll spend two nights a week at the rowing club and see if you can stick to that schedule.

- **Set up a rating system.** If you need a simple way to track your moods, opinions, and feelings about an important aspect of your goal, try rating your feelings on a scale from 1 to 5, where 1 means you're feeling unsure and uncertain and 5 means you're feeling great about it. What's your average rating for the week? How many days of the week do you give a high rating? How many days do you give a low one?

- **Be SMART about your goal.** Remember what the M stands for in the SMART goal framework? That's right, measurable. You've already outlined how your goal is measurable on page 24. Now, home in on how you can track these metrics. Will you keep tabs on the number of words you've written each day so that you finish your book by your deadline? Is it the miles you run in a week? Or is it a certain number of hours and minutes spent on studying or practicing a skill?

Get a Status Update

To know how you'll reach your goal, you need to know your starting point. The following worksheet will allow you to see exactly where you stand right now and what it will take to get you where you want to be. Write down the key stats you want to track in the left column, your current numbers in the middle column, and your targets in the right column.

For example, if you're looking to get healthier, perhaps you'll use some health statistics, like your weight or your cholesterol or blood sugar levels, or you'll rate how you feel when you wake up every morning. If you want to make more time for cooking, you might track how often you wind up ordering takeout, count how many pantry items and essential ingredients you keep on hand, and record how much free time you have each day for meal prep.

KEY DATA POINTS	CURRENT NUMBER	TARGET NUMBER

How far away are you from your targets? Or how close are you to them?

_____

_____

_____

_____

_____

_____

What surprises you the most about your numbers? What hard truths do they reveal?

_____

_____

_____

_____

_____

_____

_____

_____

Do these data points change your plans for reaching your goal? Describe these changes.

_____

_____

_____

_____

_____

_____

_____

_____

Mind Your Data

Tracking your progress not only provides you with important information but also motivates you. Think about those popular fitness trackers and pedometers you see on smart watches and cell phones. Conventional wisdom from the fitness world is to take 10,000 steps a day to maintain good health. While that ideal number has been debated, those pedometers have made it easy to track your steps and decide what to do to meet your target. Made it to 10,000 steps? Hooray! Or didn't make it? If there's still time, you might take another walk later in the day. If the day's over, you might feel compelled to take a long stroll tomorrow morning to reach your goal the next day.

Tracking a key piece of data related to your goal helps you in a similar way. Not only will you know where you stand in relation to your desired outcome, but you can also calibrate your efforts accordingly along the way.

In the earlier Get a Status Update exercise, you thought of ways to quantify your goal. Now, you'll keep track of two of those data points as you progress toward your goal. In the space that follows, record your daily stats and add any notes about what you're learning from your data. Revisit these comments regularly as you work on your goal.

1. What data do you want to record?

_____

2. What is the target you want to reach?

_____

1	2	3	4	5
6	7	8	9	10
11	12	13	14	15

Notes:

_____

_____

_____

_____

1. What data do you want to record?

_____

2. What is the target you want to reach?

_____

☐ 1	☐ 2	☐ 3	☐ 4	☐ 5
☐ 6	☐ 7	☐ 8	☐ 9	☐ 10
☐ 11	☐ 12	☐ 13	☐ 14	☐ 15

Notes:

_____

_____

_____

_____

> **TIP:** Want to record your data digitally instead? Go ahead! Use whatever notes or data recording app to keep tabs on your stats. Then set a reminder on your phone or laptop to collect your data regularly. For extra accountability, you can use this exercise to record the times you checked your digital tracker systems.

Check-In Checklist: How Are You Doing?

Before moving on to the next phase, let's check on the progress you've made so far. Answer the following questions to assess how well you've done.

Have you clearly defined your goal? What constitutes successfully reaching your goal?

_____

_____

_____

_____

_____

_____

_____

_____

_____

How do you feel after clearing out old clutter in your physical space, mental space, digital space, and calendar? What do you now have room for?

_____

_____

_____

_____

_____

_____

_____

_____

_____

You have now thought about great things that could happen if you reach your goal. Which possibilities excite you the most?

_____

_____

_____

_____

_____

_____

_____

_____

What are the most important lessons you've learned from tracking your numbers?

_____

_____

_____

_____

_____

_____

_____

_____

Now let's see how close you are to reaching your goal. Fill in the progress bar to show off how far you've come.

□	□	□	□	□	□	□	□	□	□	□	□	□	□	□	□	□	□	□	□
5%	10%	15%	20%	25%	30%	35%	40%	45%	50%	55%	60%	65%	70%	75%	80%	85%	90%	95%	100%

PHASE TWO

PREPARATION
INSPIRATION
RECREATION
TRANSFORMATION

inspiration

"

I will find
inspiration when I
slow down and stay
open to the beauty
around me.

"

After the Preparation phase, you've cleared your spaces, set some boundaries, gathered your tools, and collected some data. Now it's time to move on to Inspiration—the phase of the Elevation Approach that helps you observe your surroundings and stir your imagination.

The Inspiration phase will encourage you to find the beauty and novelty in your everyday life. Inspiration can be found in people, places, things, art, or even your everyday routines. It's how you seek out new knowledge, listen to the people around you, and appreciate the wonders of our world.

In this phase, you'll complete some exercises that will help you tune in to inspiration wherever you may find it—whether you're sitting on a bus or are on a vacation way off the grid. You'll practice paying attention and tuning into those things that stir your senses. You'll also learn to use inspiration wisely, to stay open to new ideas but also to manage what sort of influences you take in.

You'll then work on activities related to these three principles: **create rituals, build your tribe,** and **make deposits before withdrawals.**

- By creating a ritual, you will make space for yourself to tune out distractions and tune in to something that brings joy.

- By building a tribe, you'll surround yourself with people who can inspire and support your journey to work-life harmony.

- By paying attention to the deposits and withdrawals you make in your relationships, you will learn how to manage the time and energy you give to and receive from others. It's easy to take more than you can give to others, especially when you're asking the people around you for their time, energy, and wisdom. By giving before receiving, you'll keep your relationships balanced and avoid losing sight of your own ideas.

To get started with the Inspiration phase, you'll do the following:

- Write down any thoughts or feelings you have as you enter the Inspiration phase.

- Gather and catalog all your sources of inspiration.

- Curate your sources of inspiration so that you're getting the ideas and information that will best serve you.

Grab your pens and pencils, and let's begin.

Journey Journal

Before we get started with Inspiration, take some time to jot down any feelings and thoughts you have right now. Here are some prompts for you to ponder:

Some say being a lifelong student is the key to longevity. How can you keep learning throughout your life?

_____

_____

_____

_____

_____

_____

_____

_____

_____

Where do you usually feel the most inspired? What are your go-to sources for new ideas?

_____

_____

_____

_____

_____

_____

_____

_____

_____

Who in your life inspires you?

_____

_____

_____

_____

_____

_____

_____

_____

_____

_____

_____

_____

Where in your daily life could you use more inspiration? Is there an area of
your life where you could benefit from trying a new approach or a new way
of doing things?

_____

_____

_____

_____

_____

_____

_____

_____

_____

_____

Inspiration Curation

We often have many sources of inspiration beaming down on us, no matter where we are or what we are doing. Everything, from the people we meet to the places we go to the sounds we listen to, can influence our behavior. That's why it's important to make sure the inspiration we take in prompts us to do things we actually want to do. Being mindful about our sources of inspiration makes it easier to seek out content that makes us feel good and helps us stay away from anything that is unhelpful or distracting.

Using the following chart, catalog the types of inspiration you take in regularly. The left column provides categories to organize your information, but feel free to add your own categories using the blank spaces. In the middle column, list the creative influences you consume regularly. In the right column, assess what you're learning from each of these sources. Write down what feelings or new information you take in from these sources of content, even if it's knowledge or emotions that are unnecessary or unwanted.

For example, when you look at your daily news source, think about the kind of information you're finding there. Do you gravitate toward current events? Or do you click on the articles in the arts and culture sections first? How do you feel about the information you take in—do you feel informed and more knowledgeable, or more fearful or alarmed about the world around you? What do you usually learn from the stories that you read?

CONTENT	CREATORS
Art	
Books	
Music	
Podcasts	
Places	
People	

WHAT I DISCOVER

Now, conduct an audit of your sources of that inspiration. Consider which ones you want to keep seeking out as you're working toward your goal. What information would help you get closer to it? For example, would you listen to more experts in a chosen field? Or would you ask for advice from people who have done the thing you're hoping to do?

Next, think about how those sources make you feel. Do the news articles you read make you feel more informed about the world around you? Or do you feel a bit hopeless after taking in the stories? What makes you feel empowered? What will help you feel at your best and most capable for the work ahead?

After thinking about these questions, highlight or circle the three most helpful sources of inspiration from your list on pages 80–81. Then cross out any sources that will not be useful to you right now. Are there any areas where you need to find more relevant resources?

As you move forward with the Inspiration phase, return to this list to remind yourself which sources will spark your creativity.

Do One Thing

One way we can invite more inspiration into our lives is to learn to pay attention. In a world where we're constantly multitasking or overloading our senses with stimuli, our minds flit between one thing and several other things. Sure, a scenic fall walk through a tree-lined park is inspiring, but if you're on your phone swiping your social media while you walk, you'll might miss the oranges and reds that stir up those cozy fall vibes or you might not notice how good it feels to breathe in the crisp air.

Learning to tune in and tune out is key to letting your mind relax to make it more receptive to the inspiration all around you. This exercise will encourage you to do less multitasking so that you can be more inspired. For ten minutes, challenge yourself to do one thing and one thing only. For example, if you're going to do a workout, do the workout without browsing your social media in between your reps. If you're reading a book, sit comfortably, read the book, and do nothing more—no sending texts to friends, no emailing a client, no browsing social media between chapters. Taking a walk through that tree-lined park? Pay attention to those leaves.

Notice what is going on in your body as you do your activity. What thoughts pop into your mind? Do you recall things, events, or people you hadn't thought of in a while? Did you come up with any new ideas? Or did you simply enjoy the activity more than you had expected because you were leaning all the way into it? Use the following prompts to record any new ideas, observations, or thoughts that might have popped up.

Activity:

_____

_____

One thing I learned while completing this activity:

_____

_____

One thing that surprised me during that time:

_____

_____

One thing that made me smile:

_____

_____

One thing I hadn't noticed seeing before:

_____

_____

Your Personal Elevation Page

During this Inspiration phase, you have curated the types of content you consume and have practiced tuning in mindfully to the world around you. Now, use this space to capture any uplifting moments, images, or ideas you have developed so far. You can also use this space to record your most exciting flashes of inspiration. There are no rules here, just space for you to express yourself.

Create Rituals

instant elevation

**By making time for rituals, you ensure that joy is a
built-in feature of your everyday life, no matter how busy you might be.**

A ritual is any activity or exercise that is personal, routine, and sacred to the person doing it. Rituals give you the mental space to envision what you want in life. And most important, rituals can bring you calm and joy by helping you disconnect from the outside world and instead feel centered and grounded.

Rituals are especially essential for work-life harmony because they give you dedicated time and space to focus on yourself. Far from preventing you from spending all your time and energy on your goal, feel-good rituals do just that: make you feel good so you can achieve your goal.

During the Inspiration phase, you might be taking in exciting ideas, learning more about your goal, and discovering new routines. So it might seem counterintuitive to take time to retreat, to turn inward, just as you're starting to make progress with your goal. But doing so can help you become more receptive to the changes that the Elevation Approach will bring.

To practice this principle, you'll craft your own soul-soothing rituals and carve out time and space just for yourself.

How to Make a Ritual Worth Keeping

- **Make your ritual a routine.** A ritual should be a recurring activity in your life. You can decide how frequently you'll do your ritual, but it should be an activity that you do consistently.

- **Make your ritual all about you.** Your ritual should serve you and only you. Don't feel the need to explain it or justify it to anyone else. Practice it because you love it. That's the best reason and the only reason you need.

- **Make your ritual pleasurable.** Rituals should not feel like work. They are a form of self-care, and they should feel grounding and therapeutic. Rituals should help boost your mood or make you feel more grounded and calmer.

- **Make your ritual intentional.** Rituals should be activities for which you are fully present. Let go of those outside distractions or worries and focus solely on what you're doing and how you feel while you're conducting your ritual.

Design Your Ritual

You know you have a meaningful ritual when it involves an intentional, personal activity that is for your own pure enjoyment. Rituals should not feel like work, nor do they have to be productive. If you are swamped with responsibilities or you haven't made time for rituals before, you'll find that building one to fit your routine might be challenging. That's why I've created this easy-to-follow guide. Answer the following questions to build a ritual you can easily incorporate into your routine.

Name an activity you'd like to turn into a ritual.

_____

_____

_____

How often would you like to practice this ritual? How long will it take to complete?

_____

_____

_____

Where do you want to practice your ritual?

_____

_____

_____

What do you hope to gain from practicing your ritual?

_____

_____

_____

Do you need any supplies or equipment to practice your ritual? Are there any items you'd like to use to make your ritual feel special? Write them down here.

☐ _____

☐ _____

☐ _____

☐ _____

☐ _____

☐ _____

Practice Your Ritual

Now that you've written down your ideas for your ritual, take some time to kick back and enjoy a moment of self-care.

On page 91, you will find a tear-out sheet that outlines simple guidelines for a great ritual. Read these guidelines before you start your ritual so as to put yourself in the right frame of mind and to help you stay focused on the task at hand. If you like, post this visual reminder in the place where you practice your ritual.

The Rules of a Great Ritual

Your ritual should become routine; it is sacred and crafted for you and only you! Once you've selected your personal ritual, use this guide to set your intentions to feel good and be present in the moment.

RITUAL

R—Release the day

I—Initiate a time

T—Turn your attention inward

U—Unblock worries or expectations

A—Allow yourself to enjoy

L—Let yourself just be

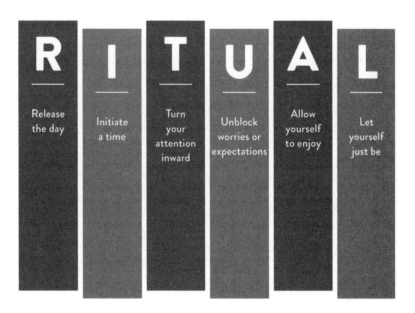

R — Release the day
I — Initiate a time
T — Turn your attention inward
U — Unblock worries or expectations
A — Allow yourself to enjoy
L — Let yourself just be

When you're done, take some time to reflect on this experience with your personal ritual. Consider the following questions:

How do you feel? More relaxed? Calm? Happy?

_____

_____

_____

_____

_____

_____

Did you allot the right amount of time for your ritual? Could you have spent more (or less) time doing your ritual?

_____

_____

_____

_____

_____

_____

Did you enjoy the time and space you created to practice your ritual? Is there anything you would change or add to your ritual?

_____

_____

_____

_____

_____

_____

Create More Rituals!

Now that you've established one ritual, let's create some more! While the main purpose of any ritual is to help you feel good, perhaps you want to create new routines that will help you prioritize a certain area of your life or will create a specific experience. For example, perhaps you want a ritual that helps you spend more time with your friends and family or you desire a ritual that helps you feel more centered.

First, gather your ideas for additional rituals.

List three ideas for rituals that bring you calm:

1. _____
2. _____
3. _____

List three ideas for rituals that help you practice self-care:

1. _____
2. _____
3. _____

List three ideas for rituals that help you feel more creative:

1. _____
2. _____
3. _____

List three ideas for rituals that strengthen your connection to others:

1. _____
2. _____
3. _____

List three ideas for rituals that can help you feel _____:

1. _____

2. _____

3. _____

Now, choose one idea from these lists and try to incorporate it into your routine. Use The Rules of a Great Ritual tear-out sheet on page 91 to help you get started. Most important, enjoy your time with the ritual and try to tune in to the experience and feeling that you're hoping to cultivate.

After you're done, revisit these questions from page 93 to reflect on the success of your second ritual.

How do you feel? More relaxed? Calm? Happy?

_____

_____

_____

_____

_____

_____

_____

Did you allot the right amount of time for your ritual? Could you have spent more (or less) time doing your ritual?

_____

_____

_____

_____

_____

_____

_____

Did you enjoy the time and space you created to practice your ritual? Is there anything you would change or add to your ritual?

_____

_____

_____

_____

_____

_____

_____

You now have at least two rituals at your disposal. Not only will they bring moments of joy to your day, but they'll also guide you toward work-life harmony. And, hey, you deserve it!

Take Yourself on a Date

Rituals are about taking care of yourself so you can feel your best. Here's an idea for a weekly ritual that serves this purpose: take yourself on a date.

Dates—ahem, *good* dates—are fun. You go to exciting places with people you care about, and you tend to put your best self forward. You might dress in your favorite clothes and apply makeup, put on special jewelry, and choose complementary accessories. But if you put your best self forward for other people, why not do the same for yourself? You can look and feel your best when you spend time with yourself. In fact, showering yourself with attention and care signals to you and others that you value yourself. The more value you place on yourself, the more you are able to treasure the things, people, and time around you. And . . . the more other people will treasure you as well.

So go ahead and schedule a date for yourself. Use this time to do something that makes you smile, such as visiting a place you love. Wear an outfit that makes you feel great. Put on your favorite shoes and bring your most treasured bag. Eat at your favorite restaurant. Go to a bookstore you love.

When you return, think about your experience. Did you have a good time? Would you change anything about your date? Do you want to try something new in the future? Keep these questions in mind as you use the following space to jot down some thoughts about your date.

_____

_____

_____

_____

_____

_____

_____

_____

_____

TIP: Dining alone on that date with yourself? Don't sweat it! If you feel self-conscious and think that people might be staring pitifully at you eating by yourself, remember that most people won't even notice you're a solo diner. They will likely be too consumed with what's going on at their own table. But if you're still nervous, try making a reservation in advance for one, or sit at the bar where the bartender can check in with you during your meal.

Build Your Tribe

instant elevation

**Having a variety of tribe members
in our lives keeps us evolving as people.**

It's important to surround yourself with good people—people who you can trust and who you know will be in your life through the good and the bad. I call these people my tribe. These are people who inspire me, who bring joy to my life, and who have supported me through thick and thin. They are the people whom I call to help me solve problems, think through new ideas, swap recipes, and share travel tips.

Now, you might have one tribe or many tribes, and each tribe may help you in different ways. Your tribe might include people who have similar goals or values as you, or you might choose to spend time with people who offer you perspectives different from your own. Either way, make sure the people whom you gather will help you with your Elevation Approach journey.

In this section, you'll find activities that will help you think through who your tribe members are and how best they can support you.

Define Your Categories of Support

When we're tackling a goal, the people around us can be some of our most powerful tools. People can help in different ways; for instance, they can offer guidance, support, assistance, information, and more.

As you think about your goal, consider what you need from the people around you. If you want to learn to code, you might seek out friends who are tech savvy and ready to help you troubleshoot errors or assist you with homework. Perhaps you might want to reach out to an old colleague who now works at a tech start-up.

As I shared in *The Elevation Approach*, I can group many of my tribe members into four categories of support: Cheerleaders, Friendtors, Board of Directors, and Fab Five. My Cheerleaders are casual friends and acquaintances who give me praise and encouragement. My Friendtors are peers and colleagues I turn to for career advice. My Board of Directors are my older and wiser friends, offering not just solid advice but also expertise and help I wouldn't otherwise have. Finally, my Fab Five are my ride-or-die friends and family members. They laugh with me, cry with me, listen to me, and help me with whatever I need, including guidance on big life decisions.

What are your categories of support? Think of a name or phrase to describe what you hope to receive from your tribe members. Then list the names of the people who fit into each category. How could each person in your tribe be helpful? Who could be a close confidante and listen to your deepest secrets without judgment? Who is always good for a pick-me-up and happy to cheer you, no matter where you are with your goal? It's possible that one person may play several roles in your life. If that's the case, add that person's name to multiple categories.

You'll use these lists in the next exercise, so bookmark this page!

CATEGORY:

CATEGORY:

CATEGORY:

CATEGORY:

CATEGORY:

Ask a Friend for Feedback

Pick a tribe member who is likely to give you candid feedback about your goal, your progress, and your plan to achieve it. Schedule the time to have a frank discussion with the person. Here are some ways you can start your conversation:

- "I'm challenging myself to _____. What do you think I can do to achieve my goal?"

- "I'm working on _____ because I think it will improve my life. Do you think this goal will help me?"

- "I've recently started to do _____. Have you tried it before? What was your experience?"

- "I am trying to do less of _____ because I think it will help me _____. How have you gotten rid of something you no longer wanted in your life?"

Listen intently to any feedback you receive. If appropriate, take notes. Try not to debate or show resistance to their opinions; instead, openly listen to their suggestions.

In the space that follows, record what you took away from the conversation. What did they say and how did you feel about what they said? Did they give you any helpful suggestions?

_____

_____

_____

_____

_____

_____

_____

_____

_____

_____

_____

_____

Tribe Tree

Creating a visual representation of your support network is a great way to see how deep it is and where you can make room for more people.

In the last exercise, you wrote down the names of some people who can support you with your goal and you thought about the ways they can help. You'll use this information to fill in the blank family-tree-style diagram on page 104:

1. First, write your name in the gray box in the middle of the diagram.
2. In the white boxes surrounding the gray box, fill in the names of the categories you came up with in the previous exercise.
3. Next, add the names of the people you listed on page 101 to the diagram using the lines that branch off each category.

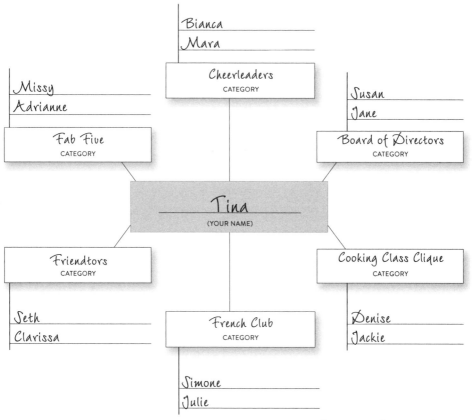

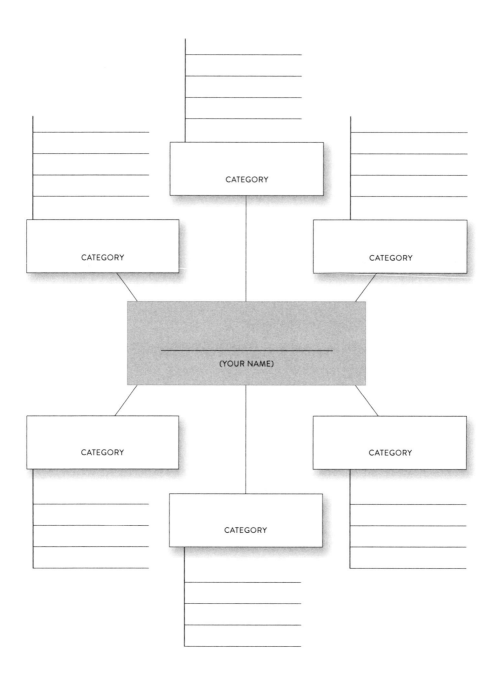

CATEGORY

CATEGORY

CATEGORY

_____
(YOUR NAME)

CATEGORY

CATEGORY

CATEGORY

Who Else Do You Need?

You've assessed who fits into your tribe and how they can support you. Now, you'll take the time to consider who else you would like to add to your tribe.

Think about who you may want to add to your tribe, where you might find them, and why each person would be a great addition to your tribe. Do you have a neighbor who is highly skilled at something related to your goal? Do you have a friend who is also working on a goal similar to yours?

In the space that follows, list the people who come to mind and the qualities that make them helpful resources or reliable sources of support.

Who Do You Need?

Name: _____

Category: _____

Their Best Qualities: _____

_____

_____

Name: _____

Category: _____

Their Best Qualities: _____

_____

_____

Name: _____

Category: _____

Their Best Qualities: _____

_____

_____

Name: _____

Category: _____

Their Best Qualities: _____

_____

_____

Name: _____

Category: _____

Their Best Qualities: _____

_____

_____

Name: _____

Category: _____

Their Best Qualities: _____

_____

_____

How to Find New Tribe Members

Sometimes, looking for new tribe members can provide the inspiration and new perspective you didn't know you were missing. But where to find new friends? Here are some suggestions:

- **Seek out people working toward similar interests.** Love wine? Maybe seek out a new friend at a local wine tasting. Have you always wanted to try pottery? Take a class and meet fellow ceramics enthusiasts there.

- **Seek out people with similar values.** Find people who have similar outlooks on life, goals, and values. For example, if you're a family-oriented person, seek out others who also consider family first.

- **Seek out people when you're trying something new.** Whether you're trying a new hobby or going someplace new, you'll run into opportunities to meet new people and have new conversations.

- **Seek out people who are different from you (or have different interests).** By finding people who are different from you—in age, in interest, in life stages—you'll foster more diversity in your inner circle.

Make Deposits Before Withdrawals

instant elevation

By being more mindful of what you give and what you receive from others, you can ensure you are putting your efforts toward the most meaningful parts—and people—in your life.

A bank isn't the only place that processes deposits and withdrawals. We also can make deposits and withdrawals toward other people, toward things, and toward ourselves. It's important to keep these transactions in balance so that we don't overdraw from others around us—or feel overdrawn by others.

A deposit occurs when you give time, energy, love, or information to someone else. A withdrawal occurs when you receive time, energy, love, or information from someone else. Deposits and withdrawals can come in many guises, whether as advice, a favor, emotional support, or a token of appreciation, such as a thank-you note.

You can apply the concept of deposits and withdrawals to anything you invest your time and energy in, including things, people, your health, your social commitments, and your information. When it comes to people, the love, help, and guidance you put into a relationship, whether it's with a colleague advising you on your goal or your best friend, should ideally be approximately equal to the love, emotion, help, and guidance you receive.

Deposits are especially important in relationships. To start relationships off on a kind, caring foot, it's important to make deposits before withdrawals. Making deposits is a way to connect with people and express how you can help or be of service to others. It also can help you recalibrate a relationship that might feel unbalanced. Have you been making a few too many withdrawals from a certain relationship? For example, have you been calling your mother only to talk about your problems at home with your loved ones and then getting off the call before she can discuss what's going on in her life? Make more deposits and you'll be able to bring it back into a happy balance. Next time you're on the phone with Mom, take the time to ask about her life—and listen intentionally to her response. Even better, offer to help her fix or improve any issue she may have at home. Is she lonely? Make a deposit in your relationship and plan a visit to see her soon. Making a deposit should feel good—it usually is satisfying to do good toward someone you care about.

Keeping tabs on your deposits and withdrawals will allow you to see where your energy goes. In the next few exercises, you'll track the deposits and withdrawals you make in your relationships and see how best to manage them.

Update Your Relationship Ledger

Do you find yourself spending more time and energy on people, things, or organizations that don't provide the same amount of love and care in return? The best way to take stock of how much energy you're putting into your relationships and commitments is to start tracking your deposits and withdrawals.

Using the ledger worksheet that follows, write down a few of the recent "relationship transactions" you've made. Think about what you're putting into the relationship and what you're receiving in return, and then assess whether these transactions leave you feeling fulfilled or overdrawn.

Want to go one step further? You can use the ledger to examine your social commitments—for example, memberships in various clubs or involvement in charitable or community organizations. Have any of these commitments left you feeling drained? Which commitments energize you?

First, here's a sample of ledger entries for someone whose deposits and withdrawals entailed being a friend, a coworker, and a helper in their child's school, along with the feelings generated by these transactions.

RECIPIENT	EVENT	DEPOSIT	WITHDRAWAL	HOW DO I FEEL?
Friend	Coffee	Listened to her issue with her partner for 30 minutes; gave advice on how to handle the situation.	Asked for help selling old clothes to clean out my closet.	Felt drained after listening to her complain, but relieved to have old clothes taken off my hands.
Coworker	Sales presentation	Prepared presentation for 2 days.	Asked her to give the in-person presentation to my boss so I could keep my doctor's appointment.	Satisfied. I did the back-end prep work, while she did the work on the day of presentation.
Child's school	Class parent volunteer	1 day/month to read at story time, help with classroom activities.	None	I feel happy and energized when I spend time with my daughter and her friends.

RECIPIENT	EVENT	DEPOSIT	WITHDRAWAL	HOW DO I FEEL?

Are Your Deposits Really Deposits?

A deposit can feel great, but if it leaves you feeling depleted and disappointed, it may not actually be a deposit. In any relationship, you should be giving your time and care to others because it feels good to do so, not because it feels good to get something in return. If you've got an ulterior motive for giving deposits, your deposit is just a withdrawal in disguise. It's one thing to help someone; it's another thing to do it simply to gain something for yourself.

To help you determine whether a deposit is really a deposit, first use the following examples of deposits and withdrawals to determine if you've fallen into the common "deposit traps." Remember, a deposit should feel good to give, no strings attached.

DEPOSIT	WITHDRAWAL
You've done a favor for a friend without expecting anything in return.	You've done a favor for a friend, expecting they'll do one for you in return.
You let a family member borrow your car.	You loaned a family member your car, expecting that they'll let you borrow something of theirs in return.
You provided a reference for someone for a job or loan.	You provided a reference for someone for a job or loan, but were disappointed when the person didn't offer you a job or money as a gift in return.
You let a friend spend a few nights at your home when her apartment was under construction.	You let a friend spend a few nights at your home, but you expected she would buy your groceries and pay your utilities for a week.
You offer to buy a round of drinks at the office happy hour for your colleagues.	You offered to pay for the drinks for your colleagues, but get angry when no one buys you dinner as a thank-you.

Now, let's get more specific. How do you know if a deposit is really a deposit? The next time you're feeling unsure, use this writing prompt to help determine whether a specific action was worth adding to your relationship ledger.

What happened with the deposit? Who was involved in this transaction?

_____

_____

_____

_____

_____

_____

_____

_____

_____

_____

_____

_____

Next, answer the following questions to evaluate that transaction. For the first set of questions, the more times you can answer yes, the higher the quality of the deposit.

Did the deposit:

Feel good to make? ☐ Yes ☐ No

Come from a place of kindness? ☐ Yes ☐ No

Help another person or group? ☐ Yes ☐ No

Provide helpful guidance or assistance to another person or group? ☐ Yes ☐ No

Improve or bring more happiness to your day-to-day life? ☐ Yes ☐ No

Require an effort that was personally meaningful? ☐ Yes ☐ No

For the second set of questions, if you answer yes to any of these, chances are your deposit might be a withdrawal in disguise. The more noes you can answer here, the more your deposits will be worth—both to you and to the recipient.

Did the deposit:

Leave you feeling stressed, tired, or overextended? ☐ Yes ☐ No

Leave you feeling any type of regret? ☐ Yes ☐ No

Leave you feeling unappreciated? ☐ Yes ☐ No

Leave you with any bad feelings about the recipient? ☐ Yes ☐ No

Make the recipient feel bad or worse about themselves? ☐ Yes ☐ No

Make the recipient feel guilty for receiving the deposit? ☐ Yes ☐ No

Come with an expectation of reciprocity or payback? ☐ Yes ☐ No

Now, consider the results. Based on your results, what would you do differently next time?

_____

_____

_____

_____

_____

_____

_____

_____

_____

_____

_____

_____

Make Deposits to Yourself

The better you get at making deposits to yourself, the more selflessly you can give to others. For one week, make one deposit to yourself for each of the next five days before you make any deposits to others. Use the following blank deposit slips to record your deposits. The deposits can take many forms, such as completing a ritual or doing something nice for yourself. For example, you might enjoy a cup of coffee and a peaceful moment before the rest of your family wakes up.

DEPOSIT SLIP

Date: _____ Name: _____

Deposit Description: _____

_____

_____

DEPOSIT SLIP

Date: _____ Name: _____

Deposit Description: _____

_____

_____

DEPOSIT SLIP

Date: _____ Name: _____

Deposit Description: _____

_____

_____

DEPOSIT SLIP

Date: _____ Name: _____

Deposit Description: _____

_____

_____

DEPOSIT SLIP

Date: _____ Name: _____

Deposit Description: _____

_____

_____

Now, turn your attention toward making deposits to others. Keep track of these deposits with this second set of blank deposit slips. How does it feel to make these deposits after putting some coins in your own account?

DEPOSIT SLIP

Date: _____ Name: _____

Deposit Description: _____

_____

_____

DEPOSIT SLIP

Date: _____ Name: _____

Deposit Description: _____

_____

_____

DEPOSIT SLIP

Date: _____ Name: _____

Deposit Description: _____

_____

_____

DEPOSIT SLIP

Date: _____ Name: _____

Deposit Description: _____

_____

_____

DEPOSIT SLIP

Date: _____ Name: _____

Deposit Description: _____

_____

_____

Check-In Checklist: How Are You Doing?

By this point, you've worked through two phases of the Elevation Approach. How are you feeling now? First, take time to assess what you've done so far.

Where have you found your best ideas during the Inspiration phase?

_____

_____

_____

_____

_____

_____

_____

_____

_____

_____

How has your new ritual elevated your daily life?

_____

_____

_____

_____

_____

_____

_____

_____

_____

_____

_____

Do you feel you have gathered the right people to help you reach your goal? How have they supported you so far?

_____

_____

_____

_____

_____

_____

_____

_____

How have your deposits and withdrawals to friends, family, and social commitments contributed to your work-life harmony?

_____

_____

_____

_____

_____

_____

_____

_____

Next, let's see how close you are to reaching your goal. Fill in the following progress bar to show off how far you've come.

☐	☐	☐	☐	☐	☐	☐	☐	☐	☐	☐	☐	☐	☐	☐	☐	☐	☐	☐	☐
5%	10%	15%	20%	25%	30%	35%	40%	45%	50%	55%	60%	65%	70%	75%	80%	85%	90%	95%	100%

PHASE THREE

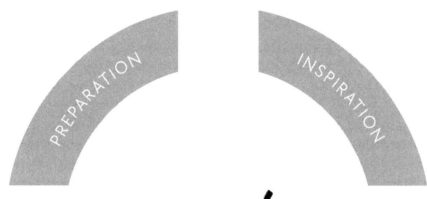

recreation

"

I embrace play and
rest as sources of
joy and harmony.

"

The third phase is perhaps the most fun part of the Elevation Approach. This is when we lean away from work and productivity, and lean into play and relaxation. This is Recreation.

During the Preparation and Inspiration phases, you might have dived headfirst into doing the work needed for those phases—collecting the data, preparing your space and materials, and gathering inspiration. Now that you're all geared up and ready to keep going, it's time to pause.

This phase is your chance to set aside unstructured time to experiment and relax. It gives you a break to refresh yourself and recharge. It offers your mind creative space to grow. It doesn't involve anything that feels like another obligation or work. I'm also not recommending you do things that are dangerous or life-threatening. By recreation I mean anything that allows you to take a breather, pause, play, and just have fun.

I know what you're thinking: *Why take a break now when I'm already this far?* Here's the simple but powerful truth: having recreation is just as important as being productive. We need to prioritize rest just like we prioritize work. So often we think that the only way we can move forward is to simply keep moving. But more effort doesn't always equal more results. Overindulgence in anything—work, training, food, spending—often leads us to feel worse. Sometimes, too much work can even lead to burnout or injury.

Rest allows us to maintain a level of moderation. It gives our minds a reprieve from the analyzing and decision-making we do in the other phases, and it lets us do nothing else but be receptive to what's in front of us. By being open to the world around us, we have the potential to encounter ideas, methods, and insights that are radically different from what we already know. We can make unexpected connections that can lead to new ideas. Play especially helps us tap into our creativity as well as lighting up our souls.

Recreation can come in the form of a break, vacation, or sabbatical. It can be as involved as a full-on retreat to a far-off locale or as simple as a few minutes of deep breathing and mindfulness. For our purposes, we're going to lean into bite-size forms of recreation—the forms that get us up and moving while still allowing us to rest.

In this section, you're going to learn about these three principles: **get outside of your safe zone, move,** and **create joy.**

- You'll get outside of your safe zone by taking yourself beyond your familiar routines and spaces. You'll explore different ways of experiencing the world.

- You'll move in any way that makes you feel good. Dance, jump, or spin. Run or do the running man—whatever works best for you.

- You'll create joy rather than happiness. Yes, there's a difference between the two, and joy is what we're aiming for.

To get yourself into the recreational mindset, you'll complete these activities:

- Write down any thoughts or feelings on your mind as you enter the Recreation phase.

- Create your personal go-to guide for recreation, with ideas for movement, games, and activities you'll enjoy.

- Practice taking a break—without the guilt.

Let's get ready to recreate!

Journey Journal

Before you get started with the Recreation phase, take some time to jot down your feelings and thoughts. Here are some prompts for you to ponder:

How can you have more fun in your life?

_____

_____

_____

_____

_____

_____

_____

_____

_____

_____

What makes you feel like a kid again?

_____

_____

_____

_____

_____

_____

_____

_____

_____

_____

When was the last time you did something just because it made you smile? What did you do?

_____

_____

_____

_____

_____

_____

_____

_____

_____

_____

_____

When was the last time you did absolutely nothing? How did it feel?

_____

_____

_____

_____

_____

_____

_____

_____

_____

_____

Create a Recreation Playbook

Play is an important component of the Recreation phase, but adults often don't make enough time for it. In this exercise, you'll use the following form to list your favorite games, people, places, and so forth, thereby creating a playbook of your favorite activities and your own ways to have fun.

After completing this exercise, you can refer to this playbook the next time you're looking to add more play to your day. Make sure to schedule time to partake in these activities regularly. Even a few minutes here or there will be long enough to bring a smile to your face.

FAVORITE ACTIVITIES:

FAVORITE PEOPLE:

FAVORITE PLACES:

FAVORITE SPORTS:

FAVORITE GAMES:

Hit the Pause Button

Part of recreation is about taking a pause from work so you can do absolutely nothing. Many people keep powering through work, school, and life until their work is done, but working nonstop can lead to burnout and exhaustion. Taking time to slow down allows you to relax and recharge your mind, rest your body, and open up to new ideas. Plus, everyone deserves a break from time to time.

Recreation is a built-in feature of the Elevation Approach because I wanted to make sure it was impossible to skip over or miss the rest stop. This break is as essential as preparing your workspace or gathering your tribe members. You should take this time for yourself without feeling guilt or the pressure to get back to work.

For this exercise, take a five-minute pause: no devices, no distractions, no work, and no studying. See how it feels. See what comes up. Then reflect on the experience by answering the following questions.

How did it feel to just simply be at rest for a few minutes?

_____

_____

_____

_____

_____

_____

_____

_____

_____

_____

_____

What feelings came up during your five-minute pause?

_____

_____

_____

_____

_____

_____

_____

_____

_____

_____

_____

_____

What new ideas arose?

_____

_____

_____

_____

_____

_____

_____

_____

_____

_____

_____

_____

Your Personal Elevation Page

As you rest, relax, and play in the Recreation phase, use this blank space to do whatever brings you bliss. Use the space to collect your thoughts, doodle, or keep images. There are no rules here, just space for you to express yourself. Or if you need a break, leave the page blank!

Get Outside of Your Safe Zone

instant elevation

Getting out of your safe zone can remove you from your work and day-to-day environment, helping you move beyond what you know and consider new possibilities.

We all have our personal "safe zones." The safe zone is anything familiar and reliable. A safe zone could be the regular route you take to work or your usual coffee order at your favorite café. It could be the same morning routine or the same job you've had for years.

There are many benefits to staying in your safe zone. It feels secure and comforting. Staying in your safe zone too long, however, can lead to boredom, rigidity, and dullness. With principle #7, you'll have a chance to explore new horizons.

Getting out of your safe zone means doing anything that takes you out of your normal routine. While leaving your safe zone doesn't need to involve any sort of physical displacement, you might find yourself going to places that you wouldn't have expected to go. And while it might feel unsettling at first, it can be done in small, approachable steps.

Making small changes like these will also prepare you for the bigger shifts that you are making with the Elevation Approach. You won't lose momentum if you take these small detours. Instead, you'll give yourself the chance to try something different, perhaps something that allows you to improve what you're doing. Sometimes, you can only see these possibilities when you step away from the familiar and expose yourself to something new.

Fight Your Fear

One reason people don't like to leave their safe zones is that they might be nervous about what they might find. Safe zones are comfortable, familiar, and consistent. The unknown is, well, unknown. It can be frightening to try new things or to go to places you're unfamiliar with, even when you know there's more to gain by doing something different.

In this exercise, you'll face some of the fears that may come up when you practice this principle. First, write down something you've always wanted to try but were afraid to, along with what scares you about doing that thing. If, say, you've always wanted to ski, is there anything stopping you from learning or signing up for a class? Are you scared of falling on the mountain?

Then think of one small step you can take to overcome that fear. Can you sign up for ski school and take lessons or simply visit a local ski resort? Perhaps there's an even smaller step you could take, such as trying on some ski gear to get comfortable with the equipment or reading up on the sport.

I've always wanted to try _____

_____

_____

_____

But the biggest fear that is holding me back from trying is _____

_____

_____

_____

One step I can take to get out of my safe zone and tackle my fear would be to _____

_____

_____

_____

Do the Opposite

Getting out of your safe zone doesn't always mean doing something big and drastic. It can also mean adding a new twist to an old routine. Here's one easy way to find that twist: do the opposite of what you normally do.

Pick an activity you usually do during the day—drinking coffee, writing, taking the train to work, or doing the dishes at the end of the night—and do the opposite of that activity. That is, if you write with your right hand, try a few phrases with your left hand. If you use a laptop to take notes, try writing them down in a notebook or journal. If you eat a certain sandwich for lunch, use new ingredients—swap the ham for turkey, mustard for mayonnaise, Swiss cheese for vegan cheese, or wheat or multigrain bread for white bread.

Brainstorm some ideas for doing the opposite by using this worksheet, then record what you learned by answering the questions that follow.

WHAT I USUALLY DO	THE OPPOSITE OF WHAT I DO

How did you feel doing the opposite of your normal routine? Did it feel awkward? Scary? Delightful?

_____

_____

_____

_____

_____

_____

_____

_____

_____

_____

_____

Would you like to practice choosing the opposite way of doing something more often or incorporate it into your daily life? Why or why not?

_____

_____

_____

_____

_____

_____

_____

_____

_____

_____

_____

Change the Venue

Another easy way to get out of your safe zone is to change the location of where you're typically completing a task. If your usual walking path is a place of comfort, what happens when you try a new route? If you usually eat lunch at your desk, can you find a restaurant or park to take your midday break?

Here, you'll brainstorm new venues for your regular routines. Using the following worksheet, write down where you normally do the tasks listed. (Feel free to skip the tasks that aren't part of your daily routine and add ones you usually do in the blank entries.) Then think of another place where you could do these things. Be open to a new approach but remember that a small change can make a big difference. Even finding a new place to brush your teeth might introduce you to something you've never seen before.

TASK	OLD VENUE	NEW VENUE
Eat breakfast		
Get ready for your day		
Drink coffee		
Work/study		
Watch television		
Eat lunch		
Read		
Exercise		
Call friends		
Buy food/groceries		
Eat dinner		
Get ready for bed		

Now reflect on how it felt to do those routines in a different place.

Did you notice anything new or different while you were completing your task in a new place?

_____

_____

_____

_____

_____

_____

_____

_____

_____

_____

_____

Do you think you can regularly enjoy some of these activities in your new venues?

_____

_____

_____

_____

_____

_____

_____

_____

_____

_____

_____

_____

Go Even Further

You've already gotten out of your safe zone by starting the Elevation Approach, creating new routines, and trying new activities. By the time you reach this phase of the Elevation Approach, it's possible that your safe zone has shifted, especially as these changes become regular parts of your day. Using the diagram on the next page, this exercise will help you acknowledge the small steps you've made outside your safe zone, will update your understanding of your safe zone, and will encourage you to continue moving away from the familiar. Let's see how much further you can go.

1. Think back to the big goal you set at the beginning of this workbook and the routines, habits, or approaches you followed before starting the Elevation Approach. These things make up your "old" safe zone. For example, if your goal is to take drawing lessons once a week, your old safe zone might have been to doodle in a notebook, a place where no one could see and critique your artwork. Or if your goal is to travel to a foreign country, your old comfort zone could have been to vacation near your hometown. List these old practices in the rectangle at the center of the diagram.

2. In the gray part of the rectangle, write down at least three new routines you've developed after completing the Preparation and Inspiration phases of the Elevation Approach. Perhaps you set aside an hour each evening to work on your goal or you chatted about your new ideas with a friend during weekly catch-ups. These routines make up your "new" safe zone.

3. Next, think of ways you can change one or two aspects of your current routines. This is how you'll be getting out of your safe zone again! For instance, you can try setting aside one hour instead of forty-five minutes for working on your goal and see how much you can still get done. Write down these new ideas in the outer (white) part of the diagram. Consider sharing your ideas with a new tribe member.

4. For the next week, implement these small changes. At the end of each day, describe your experience in the journaling space that follows. How did it feel to stretch yourself? What did you learn from doing so? Did you enjoy trying something new during this phase of the Elevation Approach, or was the change more disruptive than expected? Will you adjust your routine based on what happened?

Day 1:

_____

_____

_____

_____

Day 2:

_____

_____

_____

_____

Day 3:

_____

_____

_____

_____

Day 4:

_____

_____

_____

_____

Day 5:

_____

_____

_____

_____

_____

Day 6:

_____

_____

_____

_____

_____

Day 7:

_____

_____

_____

_____

_____

Move

Movement is a vital part of the Elevation Approach, and in this context, it means anything that gets your body in motion. It can take whatever form you want—walking, running, cycling, dancing, hula-hooping, or doing double Dutch in the park—as long as it feels good. Your body is in motion for no reason but your pure enjoyment. There are no expectations and no rules. Do whatever feels good to you.

It's important to emphasize here that the type of movement I'm asking you to do is very different from exercise. Exercise often asks you to focus on an end goal, such as losing weight or improving your fitness, or it prioritizes performance. It might also come with rules and regulations and encourages you to compare yourself with others. But with this principle, you don't need to move according to any set of rules or compete with anyone else.

As with many aspects of the Elevation Approach, movement—what it looks like and what it entails—is customizable. Do what you can with the effort that is available to you. You don't need to judge yourself or meet anybody else's standards for movement. Movement isn't what your body has to do or can't do. Your movement doesn't need to match anybody else's movement.

In this set of exercises, you'll use movement to express creativity, tap into joy, and let go of expectations and fear. You might also discover a new hobby. Have fun!

Try Some New Moves

Movement can come in many forms, can happen in many places, and can involve many different techniques. You might have favorite forms of movement, but perhaps there's something new you'd like to try. Would you like to take your yoga practice outside? Or attend a dance class at your local community center? Make time for gentle stretching before you go to bed?

In the spaces that follow, write down your ideas for new forms of movement you'd like to try. You'll consult this list and bring these ideas to fruition in the next few exercises. Remember, the goal is to have as much fun as possible!

- _____
- _____
- _____
- _____
- _____
- _____
- _____
- _____

I'd Like to Try . . .

Looking for some quick movement ideas? How about focusing less on the specific activity and more on new ways to try out something you're curious about? Here are a few suggestions to get moving and have fun:

- A class at the local park, outside in the grass
- A private session with a specialized instructor
- A dance class in a style you've never tried
- A group activity in a new-to-you venue, like a gym or studio in the next town
- An activity you have never, ever in your life tried before
- An activity that you didn't think you would be good at

Organize an Adult Field Day!

In *The Elevation Approach*, we gave you the idea to host an Adult Field Day as a fun way to play like a kid and enjoy some unstructured recreation. This activity is a great means to move your body and maybe get some of your tribe members involved, too!

In the following exercise, we've offered some fun twists on the field day that invite a little friendly competition. You can still take on this exercise solo or set up the games in your backyard or a park so that others can join the fun!

If you're hosting a solo field day, choose some of your favorite childhood activities and spend a day trying a few of them. Maybe spend a couple of hours trying to practice some of your old moves, like jumping rope or hula hooping. Challenge yourself to perfect that cartwheel you used to do in grade school. You can also consult the list of activities you created in the previous exercise to add to this day of fun.

Then, record in the worksheet that follows what you did and how you felt as you enjoyed your chosen activities.

ACTIVITY	HOW DID IT GO?

To host a field day with friends, set aside a morning or afternoon for classic field day staples, such as a water-balloon toss, a tug-of-war, or a potato-sack race. You can make it an all-day event by setting up stations for games, playing your favorite throwback playlist, and serving themed food and snacks!

Field Day Activity Checklist

- Potato-sack races
- Hula hoop
- Hopscotch
- Double Dutch
- Mini golf
- Dodgeball
- Scavenger hunt
- Water gun battles
- Egg on spoon races
- Tug-of-war

Get into the spirit of each game by recording your and your guests' experiences on the Field Day Scorecards that follow. Write down the names of the participants, the activities they completed, their personal "fun factors" ratings, and their best "scores," whether that's the number of hops it took to reach the finish line in the potato-sack races, or successful jumps in double Dutch, or the treasures found during the scavenger hunt. Get creative!

Field Day Scorecard

PARTICIPANT:_____

EVENT	PARTICIPATE		FUN FACTOR	SCORE
	Y	N	1 2 3 4 5	
_____	___	___	1 2 3 4 5	_____
_____	___	___	1 2 3 4 5	_____
_____	___	___	1 2 3 4 5	_____
_____	___	___	1 2 3 4 5	_____
_____	___	___	1 2 3 4 5	_____
_____	___	___	1 2 3 4 5	_____

Field Day Scorecard

PARTICIPANT:_____

EVENT	PARTICIPATE		FUN FACTOR	SCORE
	Y	N	1 2 3 4 5	
_____	___	___	1 2 3 4 5	_____
_____	___	___	1 2 3 4 5	_____
_____	___	___	1 2 3 4 5	_____
_____	___	___	1 2 3 4 5	_____
_____	___	___	1 2 3 4 5	_____
_____	___	___	1 2 3 4 5	_____

Field Day Scorecard

PARTICIPANT:_____

EVENT	PARTICIPATE		FUN FACTOR	SCORE
	Y	N	1 2 3 4 5	
_____	___	___	1 2 3 4 5	_____
_____	___	___	1 2 3 4 5	_____
_____	___	___	1 2 3 4 5	_____
_____	___	___	1 2 3 4 5	_____
_____	___	___	1 2 3 4 5	_____
_____	___	___	1 2 3 4 5	_____

Field Day Scorecard

PARTICIPANT:_____

EVENT	PARTICIPATE		FUN FACTOR	SCORE
	Y	N	1 2 3 4 5	
_____	___	___	1 2 3 4 5	_____
_____	___	___	1 2 3 4 5	_____
_____	___	___	1 2 3 4 5	_____
_____	___	___	1 2 3 4 5	_____
_____	___	___	1 2 3 4 5	_____
_____	___	___	1 2 3 4 5	_____

Your Movement Bucket List

Now that you've experimented with a few fun activities, try setting a few fun movement goals for yourself. Are there any skills you've always wanted to hone? Learn to do a cartwheel? Hula hoop 100 times in a row? Double Dutch to an entire verse of "Cupid Shuffle"? Learn the steps to the latest dance challenge going viral on social media?

Write down your goals using the space that follows. Be as creative, fun, and zany as possible. There's no judgment here!

- _____
- _____
- _____
- _____
- _____
- _____
- _____
- _____

Go on a Monnet Walk

If you've read *The Elevation Approach*, you'll remember how I got into the habit of taking Monnet walks when I became a member of the Henry Crown Fellowship. Jean Omer Marie Gabriel Monnet was a French diplomat, entrepreneur, and financier. Though not an elected official, he was heralded as a political visionary and is known as one of the founding fathers of the European Union. Monnet was famous for taking an hour-long walk each morning.

Today, I still make time to take a 30- to 45-minute walk each day. I use the time to listen to music or an audiobook, or just take in the scenery. These walks help me clear my mind, move my body, take in nature, and enjoy fresh air. Sometimes, I think through challenges at work; other times, I just let my mind wander.

Try taking a short Monnet walk for yourself. Go outside and walk for at least 15 minutes. When you return, use the space that follows to jot down your observations and any ideas that came to mind on your stroll. If walking is challenging for you, try moving from one location of your space to another instead. What stands out when you see your space from another vantage point?

Monnet Thoughts

_____

_____

_____

_____

_____

_____

_____

_____

Create Routine Movements

Sometimes, we can sneak more movement into our day by making the tasks on our regular to-do lists more active. Can you dance while you fold laundry? Rollerblade to pick up the kids from school? Ride a bike to work instead of driving? Walk around your neighborhood while you call a loved one?

This exercise will give you new ideas for moving more often and will help you think of ways you can sneak a bit of fun into your busy week. Mix and match various forms of movement with the different tasks you do daily. On the worksheet that follows, choose a routine task from the left column and see if you can pair it with a movement idea from the right column. Then draw a line from the task you chose to the movement idea you paired it with. You can use the blank lines to add your own ideas.

YOUR ROUTINE TASKS	MOVEMENT IDEAS
Commuting to work	Running
Phone catch-up with family/friends	Walking
School pick-up/drop-off	Biking
Listening to podcast/radio/music	Skating
Folding laundry	Dancing
Getting the mail	Squatting
Grocery shopping	Yoga/stretching
_____	_____
_____	_____
_____	_____
_____	_____

Create Joy

Joy is a state of delight and contentment. It's that deep sense of pleasure you feel to your core when you do something you love.

Joy is a key component of the Elevation Approach, and learning how to culti-vate joy will, in turn, help you create work-life harmony. You may experience many positive emotions, especially in the Recreation phase, but how do you know if the feeling you're prioritizing is actually joy or if it is something more fleeting? The most effective way to apply this principle is to recognize the dif-ference between joy and happiness.

Joy is a state of elation you feel from taking action on something you love or find meaningful. It's a deep sense of pleasure you feel to your core when you are in the act of doing an activity that brings joy, like hanging holiday decorations or taking care of your new puppy. Sometimes, you might feel joy simply by bringing the feeling to mind. As you'll explore further in The Joy versus Happiness Test on page 150, happiness is temporary and circumstan-tial. Joy, on the other hand, is a long-lasting feeling that comes from doing something you love or being in the presence of something (or someone) you love. For example, I might be happy about a promotion at work, but I feel joy at my job because it gives me the chance to be creative.

When we focus on happiness, we often encourage ourselves to chase things that will make us feel good only in the moment. These short-term things might distract us from the parts of our lives that lead to personal ful-fillment. But when we focus on joy, it becomes easier to turn our attention to work, hobbies, and interests that light us up inside, no matter what the results of our efforts might be. While happiness might be a temporary thrill, joy has the potential to become a permanent fixture in our lives because it comes from our day-to-day efforts and actions, and it doesn't depend on whether we reach a specific target or achieve a desired outcome.

In the next set of exercises, you'll find opportunities to create more joy in your life. Get ready to smile and laugh, and to enjoy the feeling of delight and contentment that will come when you've completed these activities.

Your Ingredients for Joy

Let's start practicing this principle by cataloging the experiences, actions, and items that bring you joy. Your list can include hobbies, activities, places, or people. Don't forget to include the things you loved as a child, especially if they still make you feel joyful as an adult. And remember: try to avoid scenarios that offer only temporary happiness (for example, getting a new car) and focus on situations and experiences that feel fulfilling (such as napping in the passenger seat on a road trip).

Joy Kick-starters

- _____
- _____
- _____
- _____
- _____
- _____
- _____
- _____
- _____
- _____
- _____
- _____
- _____
- _____
- _____

> **TIP:** Keep the joy flowing as you practice the Elevation Approach by making a few small changes to your workspace. Consider making your space feel cozier or brighter with decorations or desk accessories that delight you every time you see them. How about using a pen in a favorite color or sipping a beverage that brings you joy?

The Joy vs. Happiness Test

Joy and happiness both sound like things we want to achieve, but as we've discussed, there's a difference between the two. Joy is a longer-lasting state, one you can intentionally cultivate through your actions despite outside circumstances. Happiness is often a temporary feeling, a short-term reaction to a specific event.

Sometimes, it can be hard to tell the difference between the two. Eating a five-star meal might make you happy (it certainly sounds great to me!), but would you still be happy if you were eating that same meal alone after your dinner companion cancels on you or at a restaurant you didn't like? Now, think about eating your mom's amazing pecan pie. Would eating that pie make you smile if you ate that pie at home alone or at a formal family gathering?

The following are some ways joy and happiness differ.

Joy vs. Happiness

JOY	HAPPINESS
• Long-lasting feeling	• Temporary feeling
• Action-based	• Results-based, often a result of gaining something
• Not tied to specific results	• Tied to specific data or characteristics
• Not tied to specific people or places	• Usually attained when you've perfected or "won" something
• Feels good to practice	• Tied to specific people or things

To begin, practice seeing the difference between joy and happiness by answering the following questions. For each question, think back to a positive experience or situation that happened recently.

What did you feel in the moment?

_____

_____

_____

_____

_____

_____

_____

Did you experience this feeling just in your mind or throughout your body? (For example, did your breathing change? Did you feel a flutter in your stomach?)

_____

_____

_____

_____

_____

_____

_____

What memories are associated with that feeling? Are there particular people or events that come to mind when you feel this way?

_____

_____

_____

_____

_____

_____

_____

_____

What sparked this feeling? Was it because you obtained something? Because you did something? Did you feel content while doing the activity?

_____

_____

_____

_____

_____

_____

_____

Is this feeling something you've felt before? When have you felt it before?

_____

_____

_____

_____

_____

_____

_____

Did this feeling linger for a while? How long did it last?

_____

_____

_____

_____

_____

_____

_____

Would you repeat the actions that made you feel this way?

_____

_____

_____

_____

_____

_____

_____

Now, determine whether the feeling you experienced was joy or happiness. Check your responses to the previous questions by comparing them to the Joy vs. Happiness chart on page 150. Would you say that your responses align more with the qualities listed in the "Joy" column or in the "Happiness" column?

Saving Joy for a Rainy Day

In this exercise, you'll practice finding joy, even in the face of sadness or disappointment. Imagine you're in a tough situation that you might come across in your everyday life: you fall ill with a cold, your car breaks down, your friend cancels on a trip you've planned for months. Where can you turn to make yourself feel a little bit more joyful? Is it listening to your favorite playlist, watching videos starring cute animals, or picking up a soothing book? Can you use any of the items from your list on page 149 to brighten your spirits in the face of a setback?

Create a list of the go-to people, places, and activities you can turn to any time you're feeling sad or low. Keep this list handy, and you'll have the tools to bring a bit of uplift and sunshine to any dreary day.

- _____
- _____
- _____
- _____
- _____
- _____
- _____
- _____
- _____
- _____
- _____
- _____
- _____
- _____
- _____
- _____
- _____

Check-In Checklist: How Are You Doing?

By now, you've gotten through three phases of the Elevation Approach. How are you feeling about it? First, take some time to assess what you've done so far.

How do you feel after taking this time to rest and have fun? What changes have you noticed?

_____

_____

_____

_____

_____

_____

_____

_____

_____

How have you gotten out of your safe zones? What have you learned about yourself by stepping outside of them?

_____

_____

_____

_____

_____

_____

_____

_____

_____

What were your favorite forms of movement? How can you practice them more regularly?

_____

_____

_____

_____

_____

_____

_____

_____

What new sources of joy have you discovered? How can you make more room for joy in your daily routine?

_____

_____

_____

_____

_____

_____

_____

_____

Next, determine how close you are to reaching your goal. Fill in the following progress bar to show off how far you've come.

□	□	□	□	□	□	□	□	□	□	□	□	□	□	□	□	□	□	□	□
5%	10%	15%	20%	25%	30%	35%	40%	45%	50%	55%	60%	65%	70%	75%	80%	85%	90%	95%	100%

PHASE FOUR

Affirmation

"

I invite change to
bring me new
opportunities and
blessings.

"

Welcome to the fourth phase of the Elevation Approach: Transformation. This phase is when you assess what you've done to move forward toward your goal and decide what your next moves will be. This is where you will take action—and determine whether taking action means moving forward or moving on.

Transformation involves change, but change doesn't always manifest in the way we expect. You don't need to become an entirely different person or force your plans to magically come together. You also don't need to be successful or achieve your goal to undergo transformation. It can come from falling short of your goal, discovering that your current path no longer works for you, or figuring out what you don't want.

The Transformation phase offers a catalyst for change. And changes that happen because of the Elevation Approach take one of the following two paths: (1) you've made progress toward your goal, and you decide to keep going; or (2) you decide to stop—and perhaps do something else. Both outcomes are equally valuable, and each will guide you closer to work-life harmony by showing you the things you truly desire and the things that will improve your life and bring fulfillment.

To figure out what change looks like for you, you'll take time here to reflect on your actions up to this point. You'll sit down and ponder how you feel about the progress you've made. You'll ask if your actions have gotten you closer to work-life harmony. After careful reflection, you'll have the knowledge to help you make the best decisions for you and your situation. Whether it's moving forward and moving on, or letting go and pivoting to another goal, you'll do so knowing you've done the work to get this far and that your next move will come from a place that feels good in your mind, body, and soul.

As you tackle this last phase of the Elevation Approach, know that there are no right or wrong answers and that success doesn't depend on achievement. What matters most in the Transformation phase is taking the time to examine what you truly want and ensure that your actions align with your wants.

In this section, you'll learn about these three principles: **find a spiritual practice, make space for reflection,** and **let go of what no longer serves you.**

- Without a routine check-in with your spirit and values, the Elevation Approach will not be effective. But by creating a spiritual practice, you'll get real about your personal beliefs and assess whether your actions align with them.

- When you make space for reflection, you'll give yourself the opportunity to take a close look at your efforts, evaluate the results, and apply any lessons you've learned to future pursuits—all without beating yourself up over mistakes.

- After your deep reflection, you'll discover that there are some parts of your life, such as social commitments, people, habits, and routines, that are holding you back. With the final principle of the Elevation Approach, you'll learn how to relinquish these things, even when it's hard to do so.

Before you dive into this phase, here are a few exercises to get you in the Transformation mindset:

- Write down any thoughts or feelings on your mind as you enter the Transformation phase.

- Reassess your goal.

- Choose whether to keep going with your goal or change any of your plans.

Now, get ready to make more progress toward elevating your life.

Journey Journal

Before you get started with Transformation, here are some questions for you to ponder:

How has your experience with the Elevation Approach been so far? Be honest!

_____

_____

_____

_____

_____

_____

_____

_____

_____

_____

Do you think you're closer to reaching work-life harmony than you were before you started the Elevation Approach? Why or why not?

_____

_____

_____

_____

_____

_____

_____

_____

_____

_____

How do you feel about your goal? Do you still want to pursue it?

_____

_____

_____

_____

_____

_____

_____

_____

_____

_____

_____

_____

_____

Do you have other goals you want to pursue with the help of the Elevation Approach?

_____

_____

_____

_____

_____

_____

_____

_____

_____

_____

_____

_____

Is Your Goal Still SMART?

Before you begin reflecting and assessing your progress, let's revisit why you embarked on the Elevation Approach in the first place and take a second look at that important goal you set at the beginning of this workbook for creating work-life harmony.

Here, you'll reexamine your answers to the SMART goals worksheet on page 24. Use the following questions to compare where you started with where you are now. Look at how you described the goal in the beginning, then consider any new information you've learned about your goal, any joyful routines you've created, and your feelings now about your goal. You might be surprised to see how much has changed since you first defined your goal!

- Consider the **specificity** of your goal: Does the way you initially described your goal still resonate with you? Have any details changed since then? Do you need to amend or refine these details?

- Consider how you are **measuring** your goal: Is the way you're tracking your progress giving you the information you need? Have you been collecting data about your goal? What is it telling you?

- Consider how **achievable** your goal is now: Do the actions that you still need to take feel doable? Do you feel good continuing to do this work? Are there any changes you want to make to your goal or your work so it is easier to achieve and more enjoyable?

- Consider if the goal remains **relevant**: Will your goal still have a positive impact on your life? How so? How do your results so far compare with your expectations?

- Consider your **time frame** for completing your goal: Are you meeting the deadline you gave yourself to meet the goal? If not, does your initial time frame still seem realistic? Do you need to tweak or adjust your deadline moving forward?

In the SMART goal worksheet on the next page, write down your response to each question using the corresponding space. If you need to adjust the description of your goal, use the writing space at the bottom of the worksheet. Take note of what needs to change to ensure that your work with the Elevation Approach still aligns with your vision for work-life harmony and what it means to you.

S	

M	

A	

R	

T	

〜〜〜〜〜〜〜〜〜〜〜〜〜〜〜〜〜〜〜〜〜〜〜〜〜〜〜〜〜〜

GOAL

COMPLETED BY

Transformation Tune-Up

You might have an idea of the things you'd like to tweak as you enter the last phase of the Elevation Approach. If so, now's the time to brainstorm what you'd keep, what you'd like to change, and what you can do without. Using the following worksheet, write down the tasks you are completing to reach your goal in the left column; decide whether you'd like to keep, outsource, or adapt the task in the center column; and in the right column, describe what your next steps for this task will be.

For example, say you're learning a new sport. Here is what the worksheet for this goal might look like:

TASK	KEEP/DELETE/ OUTSOURCE/ADAPT	ACTION ITEMS
Take group lessons twice a week	Adapt	Sign up for private lessons. Research instructors.
Buy new shoes	Keep	Get recommendations from instructor and other players. Buy shoes.
Sign up for club membership	Adapt	Defer for 3 months after private lessons.

TASK	KEEP/DELETE/ OUTSOURCE/ADAPT	ACTION ITEMS

Your Personal Elevation Page

In the Transformation phase, you're beginning to evaluate and assess your progress and reflect on where you are and where you may want to go next. Treat this exercise as a vision board for transformation—what's on your mind? Using the blank space, write down any thoughts or ideas, create a sketch, pin or tape photos or images, or do whatever else you want. There are no rules here, just space for you to express yourself.

Find a Spiritual Practice

instant elevation

**A spiritual practice helps you live as your best self and
stay aligned with values that elevate your life to its maximum potential.**

Spiritual engagement is an essential part of the Elevation Approach. It allows you to have a heart-to-heart with yourself. It will help you figure out if your goal will keep you feeling fulfilled, encourage you to look inside yourself, and help you stay aligned with your personal values and core beliefs.

Spiritual engagement enables you to check in with your internal compass and evaluate whether your actions honor your core beliefs. It gives you a chance to ask yourself these important questions: Does what I'm working toward still matter to me? Do my core beliefs allow me to keep going? Or should I try something else? These gut checks help you feel at peace with your decisions and actions as you move through the Transformation phase.

I'm not here to tell you what religion to practice or how often to practice. Your spiritual practice is unique to you. Your spiritual practice can involve prayer, meditation, silent thought, journaling, and/or reading scriptures. It can look like daily conversations or check-ins with your higher power or less frequent communications with your spiritual guides. It can be practiced alone or with others, casually or with reverence—as long as it helps you honor your core beliefs and assists you in aligning your head with your heart. Spiritual engagement should come from within and start with your personal values, even if you find spiritual guidance from outside sources, such as your religious community.

In this section, you'll build and incorporate a spiritual practice into your routine. You'll complete a few exercises that will help you define your core beliefs, gain clarity on what is truly important to you, and learn how to connect to a higher calling as you continue working toward your goal. Most important, you'll get into the habit of checking in with your spirit.

> **TIP:** Your spiritual practice can take place any time and anywhere you like, but I like setting aside time for prayer or reading scriptures. Dedicating a space specifically for your practice is another great way to make a spiritual practice feel more rooted, but a house of worship isn't always necessary. Small things, such as a special bookmark with a favorite mantra, your favorite crystals, or a beautiful journal, can also make the practice feel sacred.

Analyze Your Core Beliefs

The following questions will prompt you to think deeply about your personal beliefs, whether they are religious or moral beliefs, or your general views of the world. With the Elevation Approach, core beliefs can involve any aspect of your life. You may believe everything happens for a reason, children should always obey their parents, or mayonnaise and mustard should never go together on a sandwich. Core beliefs are the values by which you live and the values that shape your actions.

Let's consider a real-life example. If one of your core beliefs dictates that you should give back to others in some way, you will organize your life accordingly. You may sign up to volunteer at a local charity or join a nonprofit organization. You might even accept a job at a company that has an active corporate-giving program. You may also avoid certain choices that aren't very charitable, such as buying from certain brands or companies that don't support charitable causes. These are just some ways your core belief serves as the lens through which you organize your time and make your decisions.

Take some time to analyze one of your core beliefs, then answer the questions. Don't worry about saying the right thing or writing polished responses. The aim of this exercise is to help you think deeply about what you believe and to explore why you believe what you do.

What is your core belief?

_____

_____

_____

_____

_____

_____

_____

Where does this belief come from?

_____

_____

_____

_____

_____

_____

Where do you see this belief play out in your life?

_____

_____

_____

_____

_____

_____

How would you explain this belief to someone else? Or to a child?

_____

_____

_____

_____

_____

_____

What did you believe when you were a child? How has this belief changed?

_____

_____

_____

_____

_____

Do you think your belief can or should change over time?

_____

_____

_____

_____

_____

_____

Are you open to other people's viewpoints about your belief?

_____

_____

_____

_____

_____

_____

What do you think of people who do not agree with your belief?

_____

_____

_____

_____

_____

_____

Why might people disagree with your belief?

_____

_____

_____

_____

How might your core belief allow you to feel at peace, no matter what challenges or opportunities come your way?

_____

_____

_____

_____

_____

_____

Create Intentions

Spiritual practice comes with, well, practice. One way to both form core beliefs and reinforce them is to repeat them to ourselves. This can help solidify their messages in our minds and make them second nature.

In this exercise, you'll ingrain these core beliefs in your psyche by creating intentions. Intentions are statements that declare how you want to feel or what you want to do at a particular time. I use intentions for everything that needs my time and attention. They serve as a reminder of why something is important for me. For example, when I attend a yoga class, my intention is to let go of outside distractions and relax. I set intentions when I go to work meetings to motivate my team to tackle a particular challenge or get clarity on a particular idea. I even set intentions for my family vacations—whether it's to be present with loved ones I don't get to see much or to simply to be open to the unknown and unexpected.

Here are some examples of great intentions whenever you want to tap into some positive, hopeful energy:

- I will be open to the lessons that the world has in store for me today.

- I will look for joy everywhere I go.

- I am calm, patient, and forgiving. I will forgive myself for mistakes and view them as learning experiences.

- I will cultivate good energy and radiate this good energy toward others.

Use the prompts that follow to start crafting your own intentions. Finish the statements and envision the personal values you want to hold true.

I have the ability to _____ to/for myself.

I will do _____ to feel like my best self today.

I hold _____ to be the biggest priority in my life.

I am open to _____.

I am willing to _____ in order to grow and thrive.

Now, use the lines that follow to create your own intentions. Describe what you want to achieve or cultivate as you go through your day.

_____

_____

_____

_____

_____

_____

_____

_____

_____

_____

_____

_____

_____

_____

_____

_____

_____

_____

_____

_____

_____

Elevate Yourself—and Others—with Your Core Beliefs

Core beliefs create the framework for our actions. If we believe deeply that, say, we never ask a favor from anyone because we'll forever be indebted to them, then that will determine how we create relationships with other people and how much we rely on other people to support us.

Now that you've dug deeper into one of your core beliefs in the previous exercise, you can start thinking about how you can apply those core beliefs to cultivate work-life harmony—and perhaps how you can bring more harmony to the people around you. When you're doing things that create more joy around you, you're more likely to create joy for yourself, too. Answer the prompts that follow to get a sense of how influential this core belief has been on your life.

What is your core belief?

_____

_____

_____

_____

How does it influence the way you make personal decisions?

_____

_____

_____

_____

How does it influence your relationships with other people?

_____

_____

_____

_____

Has your core belief ever prevented you from pursuing something that would cultivate work-life harmony? Has it helped you move closer to work-life harmony?

_____

_____

_____

_____

_____

Has it propelled you toward something you wanted?

_____

_____

_____

_____

_____

How does your core belief impact the world around you?

_____

_____

_____

_____

_____

Would you change your core belief in any way after completing this assessment?

_____

_____

_____

_____

_____

Your Core-Beliefs Alignment Guide

Do the actions that you've taken as part of the Elevation Approach still align with your core beliefs, especially now that you're in the Transformation phase? Let's take a look. Consider the steps you've taken toward your goal so far. Using the worksheet that follows, write down some of your beliefs in the first column. These beliefs should be ones that are relevant to your goal. They can be beliefs that you have always had or new ones that you've developed after completing the previous exercises.

Next, list the past and current actions that you've taken. Do these actions support your beliefs? If yes, come up with additional ones to strengthen this alignment and describe them in the "Future Actions" column. If not, explain what you can do instead. The more you support your beliefs with your actions, the more ease and more centered you'll feel as you continue with the Transformation phase.

CORE BELIEF	PAST ACTIONS	CURRENT ACTIONS	FUTURE ACTIONS

Make Space for Reflection

instant elevation

Looking back is key to moving forward.

Reflecting on your progress can help you achieve your goals, if done in the right way. Careful reflection helps you sit with the decisions you've made and hold yourself accountable to them. It involves taking a close look at how far you've come, what it took for you to get here, and the lessons you've learned along the way. It gives you time to think about how you've felt during each phase and how you can apply some of those lessons to your next steps. It also allows you to plot your next moves with peace of mind and will prevent you from making plans and important decisions haphazardly.

Effective reflection starts by taking a thorough look at the work you've done so far, as well as its effects. It's important to remain open and objective and to avoid criticizing yourself too harshly as you evaluate your results. For example, you might look back at your effort to learn a new language and think that you didn't succeed at it, simply because you're still not a fluent speaker. But once you reflect on what you've learned so far, you may find you've successfully managed to learn some key conversational phrases. You might even find you know enough of the language to communicate when you travel to countries where it's spoken. Viewed in this way, your efforts did achieve some success, even if it's not the success you envisioned.

In fact, rather than searching for the right answers and the correct solutions to every challenge, this is the opportunity to ask yourself more questions.

Use this time to judge less and think more. It's okay to feel uncertain and be unsure of where to go next in the Elevation Approach. What matters most is giving yourself the space to think about what has worked as you have reached for your goal, as well as what hasn't worked, so that you can move toward the former and step back from the latter.

In the following pages are a set of exercises that encourage reflection. They will help you be honest with yourself, get you to look at the bigger picture, and make sure your progress puts you on the path to work-life harmony. Plus, you'll also have the chance to celebrate your small wins. After all, you deserve it!

> **TIP:** Reflecting on your actions can be an intimidating prospect. Before you sit down to work on these exercises, come up with at least one positive statement that's unrelated to your work so as to get your mind moving in a positive direction. Something as simple as "I'm proud of myself for doing this work" can be enough to set an encouraging tone.

Look in the Mirror

If you want an accurate reflection of yourself, nothing comes closer than sitting in front of a mirror and looking yourself in the eye. Here, I'm offering a figurative mirror. Reflect on your current state of being and express yourself in words or in pictures. Think about the words or images you'd use to describe yourself right now. You can be as abstract or as literal as you like.

If you need a place to start, consider the emotions you're feeling and the intentions you might have set for yourself (see page 175). Then describe or draw those thoughts and feelings. You can also describe or draw how you see yourself or anything that represents how you're currently feeling. Be as descriptive and as creative as you want.

Celebrate the Small Wins

When we work on big goals, we focus so often on the final outcome of our efforts that we overlook the hard work it takes to get there. Noting and commemorating small moments of success reassures us that the actions we've taken so far have been the ones worth taking, and they motivate us to keep going.

In the Mind Your Data exercise (see page 69), you started tracking the numbers related to your goal. By now, you may have hit some targets, made some progress, and gotten further along than you expected. Let's celebrate those small achievements you've made so far.

Gather your latest numbers and keep them on hand as you answer the following questions.

What have you learned about yourself as you worked on your goal?

_____

_____

_____

_____

_____

_____

_____

What's your biggest accomplishment so far? Why does it make you proud?

_____

_____

_____

_____

_____

_____

_____

What new skill or piece of information have you learned from working on your goal?

_____

_____

_____

_____

_____

_____

_____

What new inspiration have you gotten from working toward this goal?

_____

_____

_____

_____

_____

_____

_____

What have you fixed or improved since taking on this goal?

_____

_____

_____

_____

_____

_____

_____

Conduct a Feed-Forward

For some, the idea of feedback is scary. Whether it comes in the form of a performance review at work or a comment from a loved one about our behavior, feedback is sometimes associated with criticism and negativity.

Feed-forward is a concept I have revisited many times in my life. I first learned about it when I was teaching at the Wharton School of Business. It was developed by executive leadership coach Marshall Goldsmith, and its main premise is to gather insights about how we can approach future situations more effectively. A feed-forward process invites constructive feedback and encourages us to think about how we can apply what we learn to get better results going forward.

Here's your chance to conduct a feed-forward for yourself and see how your search for work-life harmony is going. Take a few moments to think about these questions:

- What have you accomplished so far?

- How did you want to feel when you started working on your goal? How does your life feel now?

- What activities have helped you pursue work-life harmony most effectively?

- What were some challenges you faced in creating work-life harmony?

- Do the different parts of your life feel more in sync with one another?

- What changes can you make to help you cultivate work-life harmony?

- How could you get even better results the next time you use the Elevation Approach to work toward your goal?

- What's one thing you can do immediately to support work-life harmony?

Using the following space, write your feed-forward assessment based on the prior questions and make sure to include helpful guidance to move forward as you near the final stretch of the Elevation Approach.

_____

_____

_____

_____

_____

_____

_____

_____

_____

_____

_____

_____

_____

_____

_____

_____

_____

_____

_____

_____

_____

_____

_____

_____

_____

_____

Let Go of What No Longer Serves You

instant elevation

Cutting ties to things that aren't uplifting your life makes room for the things and people that do.

This last principle of the Elevation Approach helps you relinquish anything that will no longer lead you to work-life harmony. Letting go is hard. But sometimes it's better to let go and allow something better to come your way.

You can let go of anything that no longer helps you feel good about yourself: things, people, places, activities, or social commitments. You can let go of an old handbag that has seen better days and doesn't help you present a polished look for work meetings. You can let go of a friendship with someone who dumps drama and mayhem on you. You can stop going to places that make you feel sad or depressed, you can let go of activities that make you more stressed or sad, and you can step down from responsibilities that are a bigger frustration than they are fulfilling.

You can even let go of intangible things, like dreams or goals that no longer align with your needs. Say, you had a goal to be president of a social club you belong to. But by pursuing this goal, the time you spend enjoying the company of the club's members has dropped, and recent changes in your family obligations have made your schedule even more tightly packed. You know you'd need to dedicate at least ten hours a week to the role. You could either find those hours in your schedule to make it work or you could keep your current schedule and let go of the prospect of being the president. If you feel more at peace with maintaining your current commitments, then letting go might be the best choice.

There are several ways you can say good-bye to something that is no longer serving you:

- You can limit your exposure to something or someone.

- You can cancel or quit something, such as a gym membership, subscription, or even a relationship.

- You can eliminate something from your possession, such as unflattering clothing or foods that don't make you feel great.

No matter which option you choose, the most important aspect of letting go is being confident in the decision and walking away knowing you're making space for something even better. Sometimes, as the old adage goes, less is more. When you decide to let go of what no longer serves you, remind yourself that you're making this decision to align yourself with your highest state of harmony. You're letting go to feel lighter and more in tune with your priorities.

The exercises that follow will help you put this principle into action, with no guilt or judgment. Let's dive in.

Know When It's Time to Let Go

It can be hard to figure out when it's time to let go. Answer the following questions to evaluate whether it's time to say good-bye and move on. If you answer no to most of these questions, then it might be time to say good-bye to whatever's no longer serving you.

Do you enjoy the thing, person, or experience? ☐ Yes ☐ No

Do you enjoy the idea of the thing, person, or experience? ☐ Yes ☐ No

Are you spending time and/or money keeping this thing in your life that you'd rather spend on something else? ☐ Yes ☐ No

Is this thing or person giving you joy on a regular basis? ☐ Yes ☐ No

Are the emotional deposits you're making to this thing or person equal to the withdrawals you get from them? ☐ Yes ☐ No

Visualize your life without the thing. Would you be sad without it? ☐ Yes ☐ No

Do you think you'll find work-life harmony by keeping this thing in your life? ☐ Yes ☐ No

Sometimes what no longer serves us could better serve someone else. Answer these three questions to see if something that you're letting go could be of service to someone else. You might feel a sense of relief and satisfaction of relinquishing an item, role, or activity to a person who could get more out of it.

If this thing is an object, could someone else make better use of it? ☐ Yes ☐ No

If the thing is a time commitment or role, could someone else be a better fit for it? ☐ Yes ☐ No

If the thing is a person, could they be a better partner, friend, or adviser to someone else? ☐ Yes ☐ No

Break Up with Your Chin Up!

Breaking up is hard to do. No matter whether you're breaking up with a person, an important item, or a valued service, you might feel a pang of regret or sadness. Here, you'll practice how to break up with a stiff upper lip. This exercise will help give you closure and double down on why you're letting go and moving on.

Start by writing a letter saying good-bye to the thing (or person) you've let go of. Make sure to explain why you're letting go. For example, has it left you disappointed? Is it no longer supporting the way you live your life now? Is it not in line with your core beliefs? Writing your feelings down about letting go of the thing is not only therapeutic; it can also offer clarity for your decision.

Dear _____

Thank you,

_____

[Signature]

Next, use the contents of this letter to create a plan for letting go, using the space provided. There are several ways to approach it:

- Reduce your time and exposure to the thing you no longer need. How can you spend less time with the thing that no longer serves you? Can you make fewer visits to a business that you no longer feel provides quality service? Can you accept fewer invitations to particular social outings that leave you feeling emotionally or financially drained?

- Quit and stop giving attention to the thing. How can you stop showing up for something you don't need? Can you step down from your role on a committee or board? Can you end a subscription or membership for a service you no longer need?

- Eliminate the offending object or person from your life. Can you simply toss out or remove things that no longer serve you? Can you sell a piece of furniture taking up valuable room in a particular part of your home? Can you remove certain vices—alcohol, cigarettes, sugary foods—from your daily routine if you're trying to avoid them?

_____

_____

_____

_____

_____

_____

_____

_____

_____

_____

_____

_____

Words to Help You Let Go

Letting go is hard to do, and finding the words to tell someone or something that you're saying good-bye can be difficult.

The following scripts are templates you can use. Fill in the blanks with whatever feels relevant to you and your situation. Perhaps this is something you just repeat to yourself to help you move on with more confidence or it's something you can say out loud to someone else.

[Scripts]

1. I know that we've been together for a long time, but the time has come for us to go our separate ways. We've had some great moments together, but now I'm headed on a different path. I need to _____, and in order to achieve that, I need to _____. I'm sure you have things that are top priority for you as well, so to give us the freedom and space to do what we want, let's part ways here. I appreciate what we've done together, but I'm eager to see what we can do apart.

2. I know I've dedicated a fair amount of time and energy to _____, but now my priorities have changed. I need to put _____ first, and step away from _____. By letting go of _____, I'm making more space for the things I really need to prioritize in my life.

3. Change is a good thing. I have changed. Therefore, I need to let go of _____. I need new things in my life now that help bring me to peace, and those things don't include _____. I'm grateful for what I've learned from having you in my life, but now I must move on.

4. Trying new things is what keeps us open to new ideas. Now, I need to try something new. I'm going to let go of _____ to open myself up to new experiences. I've learned a lot from our time together, but I'm ready to learn more along a different path.

Now, take a moment to reflect on what you want to make room for, as you've let go of what no longer serves you. What new experiences can you **embark** on because you now have that time or freedom? What new people or **groups** of people do you want to meet?

Write down your thoughts in the space that follows, and get excited about what new things you now have room for in your life!

_____

_____

_____

_____

_____

_____

_____

_____

_____

_____

_____

_____

_____

_____

_____

_____

_____

_____

_____

_____

_____

_____

_____

_____

_____

_____

_____

_____

_____

_____

Plan a Good-Bye Celebration

When you decide to let go of something that no longer serves you, it's important to do so in a way that helps you feel at peace with that decision. Though losing something that was once important to us can be hard, good-byes don't have to be sad or somber events. Create a joyous bon voyage and recognize that you have taken a big step forward by letting go of something that no longer serves you.

Your good-bye celebration can be as grand or as solemn as you like. What matters most is feeling free of any guilt or regret concerning your decision. Your celebration should leave you feeling confident and secure, knowing that you've made the right move.

Here are a few ideas to get you started:

- **Pick a good-bye theme song.** Picking a good-bye theme song can be a lighthearted way to say so long to what you no longer need. You can choose something fun and catchy, with good-bye–themed lyrics, or something that symbolizes freedom and lightness. Either way, pick something that will make you feel good when you sing, play, or hum the song.

- **Set aside a day of mourning.** When letting go of something important, such as a relationship or a meaningful job, you might want to designate a whole day to grieve. Doing so will allow you to process any feelings about the loss, which will help you eventually leave the worry or distress behind. You can also use the time to write down your feelings or call a friend. When your day is done, promise yourself that you will move forward, toward the better things.

- **Practice a good-bye meditation.** Close your eyes. Take a deep breath and say to yourself, "I let go and feel good." Release the breath. Repeat as many times as you like. Open your eyes and smile, then move on with your day.

- **Post a good-bye selfie.** Dumping an old item that no longer serves you? Take a photo of the item, along with you waving good-bye, and send it to a friend. It'll serve as evidence that you've gotten rid of the thing that's no longer serving you, and your picture will also serve as a conversation starter.

After you've commemorated your good-bye, use the space that follows to describe what you did to celebrate. What did the process of letting go feel like? How did you feel afterward?

_____

_____

_____

_____

_____

_____

_____

_____

_____

_____

Revisit your answer whenever you find yourself doubting your decision, imagining what would have happened if you had held on instead of letting go. Remind yourself why you made the decision. This will strengthen your confidence in the decision and help you move forward in peace.

Check-In Checklist

By now, you've completed all four phases of the Elevation Approach. First, use the following questions to determine how you feel about your work during the Transformation phase.

Describe any important changes you've made because of the Elevation Approach. What new skills, experiences, and/or knowledge have you gained from these changes?

_____

_____

_____

_____

_____

_____

_____

How is your goal aligned with your core beliefs and values? What new core beliefs has your work toward your new goal sparked for you? Do you have other goals that align with your core beliefs?

_____

_____

_____

_____

_____

_____

_____

How have you carved out time to reflect deeply about your work with the Elevation Approach? How have your reflections affected your decision-making and your plans for moving forward?

_____

_____

_____

_____

_____

_____

_____

_____

_____

_____

What things, actions, or people no longer help you create work-life harmony?

_____

_____

_____

_____

_____

_____

_____

_____

_____

_____

What have you decided to do with your goal? Do you want to continue to pursue it? Or do you want to do something different? Are you happy with your actions and results so far?

_____

_____

_____

_____

_____

_____

_____

_____

_____

_____

Next, fill in the progress bar that follows to reflect how much progress you have made toward your goal. Did you achieve your goal? If yes, fill in the entire bar and give yourself a high five for your effort.

☐	☐	☐	☐	☐	☐	☐	☐	☐	☐	☐	☐	☐	☐	☐	☐	☐	☐	☐	☐
5%	10%	15%	20%	25%	30%	35%	40%	45%	50%	55%	60%	65%	70%	75%	80%	85%	90%	95%	100%

the next cycle

"

I am constantly
changing and
evolving as I gather
new knowledge
about myself and
my surroundings.

"

Congratulations! You've made it through one complete cycle of the Elevation Approach! I hope your days feel more joyous and lighter, and you've had the chance to experience the flow that comes with creating work-life harmony.

Since I've put the Elevation Approach into practice, I've found that I get what I need. And what I need keeps bringing me work-life harmony. I dig into my rituals and routines to grant me more moments of joy, like sipping coffee in my bedroom before I start my busy workday. I take more time to focus solely on one or two priorities at a time, instead of cramming as much as I can into each moment. Every single day I have used some principle from the Elevation Approach to improve my life, especially when things aren't so rosy. I've revisited the principles like Get Curious or have indulged in movements to help me reset, spending more time with activities that feel good, even if they have no other purpose than to make me smile.

You've worked through a set of exercises that has helped you move toward your goal. Even if you didn't achieve your goal, I hope these exercises have brought you joy and have given you moments of elevation as you worked through them. By now, I hope you've experienced what an elevated life can feel like.

So, what now?

That answer is up to you! You can embark on another round of the Elevation Approach. Use it to take your current goal another step further, or find another way of reaching it, or pursue an entirely different goal. You can take a break and relax, perhaps returning to your favorite Elevation Approach principles whenever you need to elevate your daily life.

Whatever you decide, what is most important is that you feel confident with your decision. It's natural to feel a sense of loss if you don't reach your goal or fall short of your expectations, but regret—that "coulda, shoulda, woulda" feeling—is something you can counteract. The best antidote for regret is action, and the Elevation Approach has given you the tools to act on and progress toward something that matters to you. By completing the Elevation Approach, you gave it your all. And if it worked, that's great. If you found that it didn't work, or that your goal no longer aligns with your core values or priorities, that's okay, too. It's better to know that now, and do what feels best with that knowledge so that you can make room for the things that will lead you to work-life harmony.

To help you figure out what comes next, let's walk through the following exercises:

- Write down any thoughts and feelings you have at the end of your first complete cycle of the Elevation Approach.

- Determine whether you should move forward, take a break, or try something different.

- Reduce regret by identifying which steps of the Elevation Approach have given you clarity regarding your feelings about your goal.

- Celebrate your hard work and encourage yourself to keep going with a collection of affirmations.

Let's continue into the final section of *The Elevation Approach Workbook.*

TIP: You are more than welcome to take a pause before you continue into this next section of the Elevation Approach. Perhaps you'd like to take a break after all the work you've done, progressing through the entire Elevation Approach, before thinking about your next moves. If that describes your experience, feel free to close this workbook, take a breather, and dive into this section when you're ready.

Journey Journal

Take some time to answer a few questions about how you feel after finishing one complete cycle of the Elevation Approach. Here are some prompts to ponder:

What does work-life harmony feel like to you now? Does it match the description you wrote for your very first Journey Journal prompt (see page 14)?

_____

_____

_____

_____

_____

_____

_____

_____

_____

Has your definition of work-life harmony changed since you started working through the Elevation Approach?

_____

_____

_____

_____

_____

_____

_____

_____

How can you continue to make space for the goals you really want to reach?

_____
_____
_____
_____
_____
_____
_____
_____
_____
_____
_____

How do you want your life to feel in the next ninety days, next year, or next three years of your life?

_____
_____
_____
_____
_____
_____
_____
_____
_____
_____
_____

Pause or Restart?

Are you on the fence about whether to take a break or dive into another cycle of the Elevation Approach? Use the following worksheet to help decide what decision is best for you. Circle the statements that best match what you're feeling right now. The column with the most statements circled will reflect the option that matches your best next steps with the Elevation Approach.

TAKE A BREAK	START ROUND 2 OF THE ELEVATION APPROACH
I'm tired.	I'm proud of myself.
I'm burnt out.	I'm eager and excited.
I don't know what I want to do next.	I feel hopeful.
I feel like I've neglected other parts of my life.	Other things in my life are also coming up roses.
I'm frustrated.	I've learned new things.
I feel like something is "off" in my life.	I know what goal I want to tackle next.

Make a Big Decision

You've written down your new definition of work-life harmony. You've reflected on how you feel about your work. And now you've come to a crossroads. You need to decide what to do next.

In the space that follows, write down whether you want to continue working toward your goal, stop entirely, or pivot to something else. Don't worry; there is no right or wrong answer. What's most important is to express what your next move will be—even if that next move is to do nothing at all.

I have decided to:

☐ Start another cycle of the Elevation Approach.

- I will start my next cycle with the _____ phase.
- I hope to complete my next cycle of the Elevation Approach in _____ days/months.

☐ Take a break from the Elevation Approach.

- I will take a break from working on my goal for _____ days/months.
- I will revisit my decision to continue working with the Elevation Approach on _____.

Take a long look at what you've written. How do you feel when you review your answers? Does your decision feel good? Do you feel a sense of peace about where you're going next? If so, you're likely making a great decision for you.

Rise Above Regret

Let's say you've decided to not pursue your goal any further. Maybe you've come to the realization that your chosen goal wasn't right for you. Or maybe you haven't decided what you'll do next. Perhaps you're also feeling that pang of regret at letting go of your goal. All this is perfectly fine.

The following exercise will help you feel less regret and disappointment. It will show you how much you've already accomplished just by taking this journey toward your goal. Take a minute to really notice how you're feeling now. Acknowledge your regrets alongside the actions you've taken toward reaching your goal. The progress you've made so far might be more than you think. (In fact, seeing how much you've accomplished might serve as motivation for you to consider another cycle of the Elevation Approach!)

In the left column of the worksheet, list a few regrets you might have about your unrealized goal. In the right column, identify three actions you took toward achieving that goal and the results of those actions. By recalling and recording your efforts, you'll remind yourself how much you gave and how hard you tried. Even if you haven't achieved your desired outcome, you can still feel satisfaction about everything you've done to reach this point.

Here is how you might fill out this table:

REGRET	ACTIONS
I regret I didn't launch that business.	I registered and trademarked my business's name, looked for retail space, and launched a website landing page.
I regret I didn't take that job at a new company for a better title.	I updated my résumé and portfolio, researched the company and the job qualifications, and interviewed with management and made new contacts—all worthwhile and necessary actions to stay viable in the job market.
I regret I didn't finish the marathon.	I trained for four months, I improved my mile pace, and I have run more miles per week than ever before.

Now, fill in your own experiences.

REGRET	ACTIONS

"It's okay to . . ."

As you close out this cycle of the Elevation Approach, you may be excited and proud to take on another goal, or to move deeper into the new activity you're now enjoying. Or you may not have reached your goal and have decided to pivot, perhaps with a pang of disappointment.

No matter what your outcome is, the Elevation Approach is not simply about reaching a goal. It's also about prioritizing the things that improve your life. Throughout the approach, you've learned lessons that will put you on a track that supports achieving your dreams. And if you've made it through all four phases of the Elevation Approach, you now have a toolbox nearby that you can access anytime to cultivate work-life harmony. At this particular crossroads, you are exactly where you need to be.

Following is a list of affirmations to repeat or use as mantras so you can move forward with your next steps without worry. Review this list frequently to give yourself encouragement, and then use the fill-in prompts that follow to create your own affirmations.

- It's okay to carve out space for your own dreams and desires.
- It's okay to dream big.
- It's okay to not know all the answers, but to know how you want to feel when you do.
- It's okay to change.
- It's okay to start something, stop, and start again when you feel ready.
- It's okay to not feel like moving forward and be content with where you are now.
- It's okay to have tried something new and failed.
- It's okay to still be unsure about the future but feel comfortable with the present.
- It's okay to reach your goal and want something completely different.
- It's okay to not reach your goal and want something completely different.

It's okay to _____

_____

_____

_____

_____

It's okay to _____

_____

_____

_____

_____

It's okay to _____

_____

_____

_____

_____

It's okay to _____

_____

_____

_____

_____

It's okay to _____

_____

_____

_____

_____

Nice Work!

You've just made it through one full cycle of the Elevation Approach. At this point, you should congratulate yourself for the time, energy, and effort you've put into this new way of working and living.

It's not easy to try something new or to stretch yourself beyond what you thought possible. My hope is that you feel you've elevated yourself, that you've achieved a higher plane. I hope the many elements of your life are operating more smoothly than before. I hope you now have a road map for making your dreams a reality. And if you figure out that the reality you created doesn't fit your life, you have the courage and confidence to pivot to one that does.

The Elevation Approach has been the key to helping me find the work-life harmony I was missing in my life. I still practice its phases and principles. For example, I no longer work myself to exhaustion; I always take a pause to recharge. And when I do refocus my time on leisurely activities, I embark on them with my whole self. I enjoy these fulfilling activities more than before, and all aspects of my life feel a bit more meaningful. Work is more productive—with effective and shorter meetings and more creative output. Self-care feels more luxurious—a nightly bath is more soothing with a relaxed mind and my cell phone silenced. My weekend dates with my niece, Phoebe, include many giggles.

I hope the Elevation Approach and this workbook bring that same vibrancy to your life, where the things you enjoy in your life feel even more joyful. By now, your workbook might be well-worn, dog-eared, and full of highlighted passages and thoughtful writing responses. Good! The more you use it, the better. I hope you continue to turn to these pages to collect ideas that excite you. I also hope you use this book as a form of self-care. Review your work when you can have some time to yourself, away from distractions, and sit with the emotions stirred up by the prompts and your responses. Treat the workbook as a motivational tool to give yourself a boost whenever you're feeling a little off. Let the words and actions recorded here empower you and serve as evidence that trying something new can be rewarding.

Now that you've prioritized the things that make you happiest in your life, what do you want to do more of? Reflect on the ideas, inspiration, and activities that brought you that sense of joy, and seek out practices that support your well-being and bring you more of the good stuff you want in life. Consider this workbook your personal manual for creating work-life harmony, and the Elevation Approach an essential, reliable tool to help you make that happen. I want to hear how the Elevation Approach has helped you, and I invite you to check out our private Facebook group or join me at elevationtribe.com to continue this journey.

In the meantime, know that I'm proud of you. The Elevation Approach takes time and thought. You deserve the best life you can imagine, and my promise has been fulfilled if I've helped you get closer to that vision. Now, keep going and create the version of work-life harmony that serves you best.

NOTES AND REFLECTIONS

ABOUT THE AUTHORS

Tina Wells is a business strategist, advisor, author, and the founder of RLVNT Media, a multimedia content venture that brings culture-shifting storytelling and beloved products to market through innovative partnerships. In 2023, she released *The Elevation Approach*, which shares a framework for finding work-life harmony that she developed while confronting her own professional and personal burnout, as well as a corresponding product line at Target. Tina is also the author of the bestselling tween fiction series Honest June, Mackenzie Blue, and The Zee Files, as well as the marketing handbook *Chasing Youth Culture and Getting It Right*. An entrepreneur who launched a successful market research company at age sixteen, Tina has been recognized by *Fast Company*'s 100 Most Creative People in Business, *Essence*'s 40 Under 40, the American Advertising Federation's Hall of Achievement, and more. To learn more about Tina, visit tinawells.com.

Stephanie Smith is a journalist, author, and editor whose work has appeared in the *New York Post*, Yahoo!, *Women's Wear Daily*, *People*, *Money*, and Condé Nast publications. She has written twelve books to date, including the popular food memoir, *300 Sandwiches: A Multilayered Love Story . . . with Recipes*, based on her viral food blog *300Sandwiches*. Stephanie is the cowriter of the award-winning middle-grade fiction series The Zee Files and Honest June. Additionally, Stephanie is a certified yoga teacher (RYT500) and creator of mindfulness games and content for young readers.